From Two Wheels to Four

Inspiring Hope through Adversity

JOSEPH S GROH

Copyright © 2014 Joseph S Groh
All rights reserved.
ISBN: 1495305414
ISBN 13: 9781495305412
Library of Congress Control Number: 2014903793
CreateSpace Independent Publishing Platform,
North Charleston, South Carolina

Table of Contents

	Dedication	v
	Foreword	vii
	Preface	ix
	Acknowledgments	xiii
1	FATHER'S DAY	1
2	COMING-OF-AGE IN THE HOLY ROMAN EMPIRE	5
3	THE CATHOLIC EXPERIENCE	13
4	SCHOOL, FAMILY, AND CAREER	25
5	THE ALLIED VAN LINE YEARS	41
6	JUNE 15, 2008	51
7	ICU AND RECOVERY	57
8	BAYLOR INSTITUTE OF REHABILITATION	65

9	HOME AT LAST	77
10	A NEW LIFE	87
11	HITTING OUR STRIDE	95
12	THE FOUNDATION	105
	About the Author	113
	References	115

Dedication

I dedicate this book to my wife, Sue. She is my best friend and soulmate, and her unwavering strength keeps me strong. She will always have my undying love. Her compassion, love, and strength in the face of adversity is rare. She is indeed one in a million.

Foreword

I came to know Joe and his story through "miraculous coincidences." Some people refer to events that bring people together at specific moments as miracles. Some call these events the work of angels. I only know these miraculous coincidences happen, and they are God's way of helping us find and define purpose in our lives.

Some readers of Joe's story might find it interesting that I refer to Joe's life-altering accident in the same sphere as a miracle. Joe's story, however, was amazing even before his accident, and now Joe's life and story definitely enter the realm of miracles.

I first met Joe at work. He was a sharp, enthusiastic, level headed, young man. Through a series of coincidences, he came to work for me. Why were they coincidences? Because he took an unlikely road to get to Texas and become involved in the heating and air conditioning industry. Yes, he grew up in heating and air. His grandfather and father both owned a heating and air conditioning contracting business, but it was a path he rejected after high school.

Joe began his young career search wanting to be a priest. He even attended seminary for four years. While it was not to be, God definitely knew what he was doing sending Joe in that direction; otherwise he would not have met his amazing wife, Sue, and had three extraordinary kids.

Joe grew up in the Midwest. A few short years after high school, he ended up where he swore he would never be, working for Lennox, a manufacturer of heating and air conditioning equipment. After a series of coincidences, he ended up working for me in Texas. I think

God was directing Joe into my life more than the other way around. In another coincidence, Joe knew my husband John before I did, having taken classes from him in Marshalltown, Iowa.

So why do I take a series of common coincidences and elevate it to a miracle? Because if God had not brought Joe into my life, I might have never known the depth of the human spirit and the resiliency that comes from a positive attitude. I have seen and heard of many people who have given up after life-changing events less catastrophic than Joe's. Joe told us a few months after the accident that he only allowed himself to feel pity until help arrived on the scene. After that he made a promise to continue to make the most of his life. And he has.

If God had not brought Joe into my life, I probably would not appreciate how important a sense of humor can be in dealing with life's adversities. Joe was once thanking several of us for helping him get the Joseph Groh Foundation underway. John, my husband, said, "Joe, if you had been in our shoes, you would have done the same thing for us."

Joe, with his dry sense of humor, said, "If I could be in your shoes, I would be on my way to a golf course." We all laughed with Joe until we cried.

Finally, if God had not brought Joe into my life, I might not have experienced an old adage my dad often used. Dad used to say, "You always know the worth of a man by how his kids turn out." Measured by that adage, Joe is one of the most worthy men I know. Never have I experienced a family come together and support one another through the good and bad of life as Joe's family has done.

People often look for and find depressing things in the news and in life. So turn off the news and read this book. When reading Joe's story, look for more miraculous coincidences, and then seek them in your life.

Vicki La Plant

Preface

I don't know why I felt so calm on that hot June day. Lying on the side of the trail, the thought of not being able to move should have terrified me. I remember wondering if this condition was temporary, and I had the urge to engage in an SOS prayer. You're familiar with those. That's a plea bargain with God about what you would do to escape your current situation. I reasoned, however, that present circumstances were too serious, and it would be improper to engage in such a prayer.

    I had always thought of a bicycle as my friend and transport to freedom. When I was in late grade school (sixth through eighth grade), my bicycle allowed me to hold down a paper route across wide-ranging neighborhoods of spread out subscribers. I delivered many papers other than the hometown *Peoria Journal Star*. My customers' morning appetites included the *Chicago Tribune*, the *Chicago American*, *Chicago Daily News*, and the *Wall Street Journal*. I needed a bicycle to cover that route, and I needed that route to pay for the bicycle. It was the first major asset I ever invested in, and it served me well. My friends and I rode all through the Bradley University campus and the city of Peoria. My bicycle was a single-speed, green Murray Wildcat. Some of my friends had the more coveted Schwinn Stingray, and one of my friends had the ultracool five-speed Schwinn Orange Krate. (It's astounding that one of those in good condition will bring about three thousand dollars today.) Being an American history buff, sometimes I imagined my bike was my fighter plane. I thought of it as an F4F

Wildcat fighter. It was not as fast or nimble as the other planes but a lot more durable. The guys with Schwinns were always tinkering with their rides, and I likened their bikes to the faster and more maneuverable Mitsubishi Zeros.

Schwinn Orange crate

Murray wildcat

I didn't have much cause to ride a bike in high school because my trusted Wildcat was stolen just prior to my freshman year. During the hundreds of miles I logged in grade school I never incurred any real injuries. I was hit by cars twice, but the incidents were pretty minor. The only serious injury I remember was when I was racing through a remote parking lot with my friend Bill Sellers, who owned the Orange Krate. We were racing for home, and Bill was fairly well ahead of me. He did not see the cement parking divider until it was too late. The impact threw him off his bike and onto the concrete, causing him to be pretty badly cut up. He also lost a number of teeth in the incident. After checking with him, I rode furiously to his house to summon his parents. I remember the grim look on their faces as I described the accident and urged them to hurry to the scene. While I never forgot that accident, I also never thought I would be involved in something like that or worse.

Back on the trail, I recognized that my present condition might be permanent, even though the word *paralysis* never entered my mind. I never gave serious thought to the fact that I might die, but I knew I needed to mentally prepare for a very different future. I told myself I only had until the ambulance arrived to feel sorry for myself. After that I vowed to never look back, never give up, and remain positive.

Acknowledgments

Thanks to the people who helped write, edit, and publish this book.

- Stephen, Eric, and Christie, who had to relive painful memories in sharing their own
- Sue, for her keen eye in helping edit a manuscript detailing a difficult chapter in her history
- Dottie Gandy and Joy Peeler, for their review of and suggestions for the initial manuscript – and for their encouragement
- CreateSpace, for their guidance editing and publishing this book
- Neil Lanctot, for his book *Campy*, which provides insight into the life of Roy Campanella and those living with paralysis before the advent of modern rehabilitation

1

FATHER'S DAY

Stephen's college graduation, May, 2008
– the last picture taken of me standing

Father's Day is one of those family holidays I always look forward to, but 2008 was slightly different. It was the first time we wouldn't have all the kids together on that day. Stephen, our oldest, was working a rail project in Yuma, Arizona, and was able to fly back for the weekend, but Eric, our middle son, could not get time off from his college job in Abilene. Christie, our youngest, was leaving for APPA, a weeklong church youth mission trip so named because the original group worked in the Appalachian area. This year they were headed to Prescott, Arkansas, to rebuild houses. The day dawned the way only a Texas summer day can—completely cloudless with bright blue skies. The forecast called for the year's first one hundred-degree day. On Sunday morning we loaded Christie's items into the car and headed for Christ United Methodist Church in Plano, where we had been members for years. We attended the 9:45 a.m. service and then helped transfer Christie's gear to the waiting APPA buses. After seeing her off, we headed back to Grapevine with Stephen to have brunch at Mimi's, one of our favorite restaurants. They were packed as usual, but we were in no hurry and enjoyed a relaxed meal. Following that we headed back to the house, and I was presented with Father's Day gifts. Eric called to wish me a happy Father's Day, and by then it was late afternoon, so Sue had to take Stephen back to the airport. I planned to grill some steaks for dinner as I typically handled cooking on the weekend. I found it relaxing, and the tradition went back to the days when we were dating and would cook for each other on weekends. Before I started dinner, I felt the need for a workout, as I had not exercised all weekend. I debated whether I should swim or go on an aerobic bicycle ride. The swimming option was attractive because the prediction of a one hundred-degree day had come true. Plus it was quick and easy. We had a pool in the backyard, so I could easily get in thirty minutes or more of swimming laps. On the other hand, I had not ridden my bike much that summer, and I enjoyed riding on the various trails encircling Lake Grapevine. The previous summer had seen floods in the area, and many of these trails had been inaccessible. I determined a bike ride was in order, so I put the potatoes in the oven to bake. I planned to be back before they were finished in an hour.

  I grabbed my headphone radio, turned it on, and wheeled my bike out of the garage. I like up-tempo music when I work out, but I was feeling like country music, so I dialed in 99.5 The Wolf. I could hear the garage door closing behind me as I mounted my bike and started down the driveway. The radio announcer proclaimed, "It's five o'clock in Texas," as I rode into the street and headed for the start of Oak Grove Trail, which was about a mile away. I rode cautiously to the trail as it involved traversing a four-lane road where cars regularly violated the forty-five miles per hour speed limit. Once I hit the trail opening, I picked up the pace to build my heart rate. A good song came on the radio, which allowed me to easily get into an aerobic rhythm. As my heart rate increased, my breathing settled into a typical workout pace. Sometimes I would not be in the mood for a workout, but once I got up to my workout pace, I would feel more energized and want to lengthen my session. This day had that feel. I was energized and clipping along at a good pace. I heard the radio announcer say, "it's five fifteen in Texas," as I rounded a curve. One of the lake bays became visible, and I saw two boats. Their occupants seemed to be enjoying each other's company. Turning my attention back to the trail, I saw a left curve coming up, and felt my speed might be too high to successfully navigate it. Years of riding this bike had taught me to brake only the rear tire in these situations to maintain control. I stopped pedaling and began to brake, but I felt the front tire starting to slide to the right on the sandy trail. I didn't want to overcorrect, as that would cause a certain accident, but I could not prevent the right tire from sliding off the trail edge.

    While all this happened in a matter of seconds, I can remember it as though in slow motion. The right tire left the pavement and plunged headlong into the uneven terrain. At that point I knew an accident was certain, and as I headed over the handlebars, I remember wondering how much this was going to hurt.

2

COMING-OF-AGE IN
THE HOLY ROMAN EMPIRE

Overcoming adversity is a destination for some and a journey for others. I once heard a sermon series by Don Underwood, senior pastor at Christ United Methodist Church in Plano, Texas, about overcoming obstacles. He linked one's effectiveness at doing so to a combination of one's life experiences, support network, and faith. That resonated strongly with me, but with all due deference to Don, I would add one more item. A healthy sense of humor! It helps everyone sharing a difficult journey take life's obstacles a little less seriously.

My life experiences, support network, and faith were intertwined with growing up Catholic among eight other siblings during the 1960s. It seemed as though all large, Catholic families moved to the same neighborhood, so just about everyone I knew was like us. Catholic neighborhoods were sprawling campuses where nearly every household was populated with multiple children. I remember a family a few doors down who wanted to have twelve boys in order to name each one after an apostle. They had thirteen children but not twelve boys. Our support network went far beyond our parents. A support network consisted of your family, your friends, your friends' parents, nuns, and priests affiliated with your school and your parish. Everything revolved around the parish

Easter 1963, from left to right Theresa, Sue, Me, Ruth, Tom, Jenny, Mary... holding Matt (George was not born yet)

The Midwestern culture in which we were raised encouraged hard work and self-reliance. Money was always tight in a family of eleven, but we had what we needed. From as early as I can remember, each sibling was assigned a particular set of tasks. Some of mine included drying the dishes after dinner, running the vacuum sweeper throughout the house on Saturdays, and raking the leaves on an impossibly large lawn with the wind blowing during fall afternoons. I remember being disappointed with the look of the lawn because of the wind. I would go inside, and my mom would point out the still untidy yard, and back I would go with my leaf rake. It was only much later it dawned on me this was a way to keep me occupied and out of trouble with my eight siblings. My mom's hearing was better than Flipper's when it came to the vacuum sweeper being engaged (or not). There were times I would leave the sweeper on but lay the wand down in order to join one of my siblings in general hooliganism. In short order I would hear my mother calling for me and asking what I was doing. "Sweeping," I would yell back while dashing for the vacuum to resume my duties.

Saturday mornings were a model of German efficiency. We each had a weekly duty that had to be completed by the time my mom got back from the grocery store. My task was to shine the family shoes. Given that each person had a couple of pairs, I had dozens of shoes to shine. Around lunchtime my mom would return from the grocery store in her white, 1959 Rambler station wagon. The backseat would be folded flat, and the entire vehicle would be filled with sacks of groceries. There were always about fifteen bags or so, and I remember my parents commiserating over the one-hundred-dollar expense that represented. While that sounds like a bargain today, it represented a decent amount of money back then. Once the car pulled into the driveway, general quarters was sounded, and everyone took their positions. First the unloading crew went into action, bringing sacks into the kitchen and setting them on the table. Next the unpacking crew quickly took items out of the bags, separating them into piles based upon where they went. (perishables versus kitchen pantry items versus bathroom supplies etc.) Then the put away crew carried everything to its final destination. Everyone knew their task, and the whole job was completed in short order.

Mealtime necessitated a certain degree of inventiveness to bring food to the table in a timely fashion. Using the standard two-slot toaster simply would not do when making toast for eleven people. My mom loaded up a cookie sheet with a dozen pieces of bread and put it under the broiler. One of us was assigned to watch the bread and alert Mom when it was time to pull out the cookie sheet, flip each piece of bread, and put the tray back in to finish. From these experiences I learned how to take large, multifaceted tasks and break them into smaller, more manageable ones.

St. Mark's class picture: I am second row, fourth from left

Sixth grade brought a number of significant changes. It seemed all the boys in my class simultaneously became aware of girls, and to make a negative, public comment about someone's girlfriend would result in an invitation to fight behind the school after class. One learned to be discerning about any comments. Sixth grade also brought the opportunity for a paper route and a janitorial job at school. Every morning my mom would wake me around 5:30 a.m. so I could begin to organize the various newspapers for delivery. Part of organizing involved reading the key stories of the day. I remember a number of mornings like the one in June 1968 as I carefully pored through the details of the RFK shooting in each of the papers I delivered. I would often read beyond my allotted time, so I would have to quickly load up the baskets on my bike and sling the two satchels over my shoulders prior to setting off. I dreaded the cold, snowy, winter days, which made it difficult if not impossible to use my bike. That meant deliveries took even longer, and my gloves never seemed sufficient to keep my fingers adequately warm.

The janitorial job was equally as lucrative as the paper route, so every day after school my friend Scott Linsley and I would dust mop, and straighten up three classrooms and a hallway. Between the paper route and the janitor position, I earned ten dollars per week, a princely sum for a thirteen-year-old.

The summer following eighth grade was even more lucrative. A classmate's father owned one of the nicest hotel and restaurants in Peoria, Illinois: Jumers Castle Lodge. One day I approached my classmate about employment opportunities. After checking at home, he instructed me to come to the restaurant's kitchen employee entrance at three p.m. the following Saturday. I was there at the designated time and given an application. Three weeks later I had not heard anything, so I decided to fill out another application. Soon after I received a call that I had been hired as a busboy, and I was strictly admonished to tell any inquiring customer that I was sixteen. On the few occasions I was asked to give gave my age, the reaction of the inquiring customer was usually a slow positive nod, a grin, and a comment such as, "Sure you are, son. Sure you are." My reaction was to move to the next table as quickly as possible to discourage further conversation. Soon after receiving the call to be a busboy, I received a response to my second application. This resulted in being hired as a dishwasher. Dishwashers were entitled to order a meal during breaks, and that was one of the best parts of the job! I almost always concluded my meal with some of the restaurant's infamous cinnamon rolls. Years later I still found their cinnamon rolls to be the best in central Illinois. Meanwhile I kept the paper route that summer, so between that and the restaurant, I was pretty flush. My parents encouraged me in all these activities, and the experience taught me lifelong lessons about the value of hard work and self-reliance.

In the organized chaos that is growing up in a large family, everyone needs his or her own time and space to get away from it all. Living in Springfield, Missouri, from first through fifth grade, our house was uniquely built to accommodate this. From front to back, it occupied a city block—from St. Louis Street to Trafficway. In 1861 the home was headquarters to Union General Lyon during the Battle of Wilson's Creek, which was just outside Springfield. General Lyon was killed in the battle, and coincidentally Lyon County, Kansas, where I was born, was named after him. The front entry featured a long, rectangular hall and made for a perfect football field. A grand, winding staircase descended into the back of the front entry hall, and it featured a landing halfway up. The landing was large enough to accommodate multiple pieces of furniture. On the walls were gas lamps, dating back to the time before electricity. The bathroom I shared with my brother had a black and white checkered marble floor that was always cold in the winter. The home was heated by a very old and cranky four hundred thousand BTUH steam boiler, which my father taught me to drain when he was away on business. I saw this as a solemn responsibility, partly because of his description of what would happen if the boiler pressure was allowed to exceed certain levels. There were three backyards, which we named "back," "middle back," and "way back." The last yard was about an acre. There was also a large, two-story barn with a double horse stall in back. Today that property now contains the corporate headquarters for hotel developer John Q. Hammons.

When I wanted some solace, I would take my latest library book and curl up on the back stairs of the house. One hundred years before, the stairway had served as the slave entrance into the kitchen. I was a history buff and read every book I could get my hands on about American icons such as George Washington, "Mad" Anthony Wayne, Stonewall Jackson, Andrew Jackson, John Paul Jones, and many more. These stories seemed all the more real given the history of our house, and they instilled in me a lifelong interest in American history. Growing up in a large family, I learned the value of solitude and entertaining myself in an interesting and educational way. These lessons have not been lost over the years.

Playtime meant anything from being outside alone to playing with a few others or half the neighborhood. Avid baseball fans, my older brother Tom and I would often head down to the nearest school to play a game we called cork ball. We would use a rubber ball or tennis ball and a hardball bat. We would draw a rectangle on the brick wall with a rock to outline the strike zone. Then we would define our first and third base foul poles as well as our markers for a home run, double, and triple. Runners were imaginary, and we would keep track of them and the score. Both fierce competitors, I had my hands full in these games because Tom was nearly four years older. Frequent patrons of the YMCA, we were very involved in their swimming programs. The highest level achievable in the Y program was "Shark," and when I beat Tom to that level, he was less than pleased. When play involved the neighborhood, there was no gender barrier. Girls played alongside boys and were given no special treatment. There were some neighborhood girls who were regularly chosen ahead of certain boys, and the only ones who objected were the boys chosen after a girl!

Despite being surrounded by legions of other kids, it wasn't unusual to find yourself outside playing alone. In these instances I would use my imagination to fit the occasion. Sometimes I would be star pitcher Bob Gibson or Jim Hart, the starting quarterback for the St. Louis football Cardinals. Other times I would be Walt Frazier, the star shooting guard for the New York Knicks. (This was only because the Knicks always seemed to be on TV) On my bike I was a race car driver or fighter pilot. In every situation I made up specific rules applicable to the event. I always wanted to win, and the only way to be fair about it was to have rules which created a level playing field. If I were playing basketball, for example, I would have to get the rebound in the air following a shot to retain possession.

I retained this vivid sense of imagination into adulthood, and it has come in handy when waiting for a medical procedure or deflecting my thoughts in the middle of the night from the irritation of an itch I cannot scratch.

Growing up in a large family, I learned everything from how to work with others to how to be comfortable by myself. It is important for people to find friends whom they can truly be themselves with, but it is most important to learn how to become friends with oneself. I can't imagine overcoming a life-altering scenario without that self-awareness.

3

THE CATHOLIC EXPERIENCE

Growing up Catholic in the '60s was a lot more involved than going to church on Sunday and participating in a youth group. It was an all-encompassing experience that affected every aspect of your life, and it certainly influenced who I became.

People laugh today at the thought of Catholic nuns rapping their students on the knuckle with a ruler, and while these incidents were true, they were also generally well deserved. Every morning we set off to attend Mass before school, and familiarity with the routine bred a sense of boredom with the proceedings. In the fourth grade, one of my classmates who had more energy and chutzpah than most, decided to channel his boredom into a game of Whac-A-Mole. He would duck down from his pew and within short order pop up into another one some ways away. Crawling along, he couldn't always tell where he was, and occasionally he would pop up next to a nun or lay teacher, who would promptly reward him with a swat. Following Mass we paraded past a stern-looking Msgr. Mahoney like troops passing a review stand, the boys neatly dressed and girls in their uniforms. My Whac-A-Mole classmate was often the recipient of additional attention during this march.

We were eligible to become altar boys in the sixth grade but only after passing a rigorous test. Mass was still being said in Latin, so we had to be able to unhesitatingly recite any prayer used during Mass in Latin to pass the test. A no-nonsense nun presided over these tests. Becoming an altar boy brought prestige and the opportunity to make a little money. Serving funerals and especially weddings was highly desirable because of the tips. It could also bring unexpected trouble from your friends, though. In eighth grade I served the funeral Mass for a murdered *Peoria Journal Star* reporter, and our large church was filled to the brim with well over one thousand very solemn mourners. This included the mayor. Incense was used at a funeral, and the round, hockey puck-shaped substance was lit by holding a match to the center of the star shape on top. My fellow altar boys were in the sacristy, and I could see them, but the public could not. They had lit a piece of incense, were tossing it back and forth like a hot potato, and making faces at me. I was trying hard not to laugh but apparently not to the satisfaction of Father Fitzgerald, our pastor who was presiding over the funeral Mass. Father Fitz, as he was known, was the product of a tough Irish Catholic family. It was rumored that would-be thieves once broke into the sacristy where they ran into him. A former boxing champion, Father Fitz made short work of them, after which he tied them up and called the police. My less-than-successful attempt to contain my composure attracted his Irish temper, and while walking by as part of the service, he managed to casually give me a good, swift kick. I promptly stopped looking at my friends, I knew they would get theirs after the service.

Sixth grade was the time of the great spitball wars. Bic pens made for the perfect musket in this conflict. One would simply roll a piece of paper to the right size and then use the polystyrene ink barrel as a ramrod to push the paper bullet inside the pen casing. The flared shape perfectly facilitated blowing the spit wad toward the intended target with amazing accuracy. Teachers understandably took a dim view of this activity, and the offending soldiers were remanded to a classroom during recess as punishment. They were told to fill a rather large box with small spit wads, and that they would miss as many recesses as it took to accomplish that. At one point we got the bright idea to fill the bottom half of the box with packing, thereby cutting our job in half. Unfortunately we were caught, and our punishment was to start over with an even bigger box. The nuns dictated the diameter of spitballs for the box, and they would stop by about three times a week during recess to measure random samples. This pretty well deterred cheating.

By eighth grade some of us decided to take up what we saw as the cool and suave habit of smoking. While everyone else was out at recess, we were smoking in the boys' room. Not thinking anyone could smell cigarette smoke speaks to the logic of a thirteen-year-old boy. Nevertheless one of us was always assigned guard duty, and we would stand by the bathroom door on the lookout for prowling nuns. Since we were in the boys' room and the nuns were female, we thought we were in a protected environment. We were wrong. One day our lookout sent the warning that a nun was patrolling the nearby hallway. He let the heavy door close, and the telltale sound alerted the nun. When our lookout cracked the door open for another peek, he saw a nun steaming toward the boys' room like a destroyer bearing down on a submarine. We all dove into stalls, threw our cigarettes in the toilet, flushed, and waited for whatever came next. Sister Viola charged through the bathroom, pulling us out by our shirt collars. Punishment was swift and sure at school and at home. Both teachers and students knew that school discipline had the support of the parents.

Sunday afternoons and certain summer evenings were for hanging out with friends. My friends were actually more than just friends because we did everything together. We went to school together, served as altar boys together, and were active in Boy Scouts together. I cannot think of a single event during those years in Peoria, Illinois that didn't involve these guys. One such friend, Mike Finan, lived on a boulevard with a grass-lined path running down the middle of the street. It served as a perfect football field. I would regularly gather there with Scott Linsley, Mike Yocum, Bill Sellers, and others from the neighborhood to play touch football. Other times we would race go-karts at the track at the bottom of the hill in Bradley Park. We always felt welcome in our friends' homes, and their moms usually had snacks and drinks for us. I still remember watching LBJ's speech in the spring of 1968 about not seeking or accepting another term as president. I was at Mike's house with his parents and several other friends.

When we weren't providing consternation for the nuns or our parents, we were learning. We learned cursive during the lower grades, diagramming sentences in the middle grades and world history and math in the later grades. Catholic schools gave us a good education and a strong sense of community in a faith-based environment.

In 1969 there was a prescribed path for Catholic students in our Peoria neighborhood entering high school (ninth through twelfth grade). The boys went to Spalding Institute, and the girls went to the affiliated Academy of Our Lady. There was one other choice, but it was almost never exercised. That was going to a high school seminary. If you wanted to be a Catholic priest, it typically involved fourteen years of study and work. The first four years were high school, and to be a Franciscan priest from Illinois meant leaving home and going to school in Cincinnati, Ohio. That is the choice I made.

Growing up Catholic had a huge influence in my life. Two of my aunts were Catholic nuns, and one uncle was a Franciscan priest. Making the decision to leave home at fourteen seems inconceivable in today's world, but back then it wasn't. It was not a decision made lightly, and it was not completely in the hands of the student. In some cases parents steered the child strongly toward or away from that choice. Neither was the case in my situation. My parents simply supported the decision that I made. I am not sure why I decided on the seminary, but I did feel a calling toward becoming a priest. All the priests I had known were kind, well-educated men of faith who were looked up to as leaders in the community. There were several steps in the admission process and not all who applied were accepted. There was an interview to ascertain your suitability and mind-set, and there was an IQ test to measure mental capacity. Of all the kids I knew, only one other made a similar choice. He was Greg Braeckel, a friend of mine from when we lived in Springfield, Missouri. Many of my eighth-grade classmates did not understand my decision, and some derided it. It was difficult to think of leaving home and all the people I held dear. Nevertheless, in the fall of 1969, I left for St. Francis Seminary in Cincinnati. Historically high school seminaries nurtured young men's vocational choices, and a high percentage went on to become priests. The late '60s and '70s, however, broke that mold for good.

The graduating class of '73 was twenty-eight members strong, representing about half as many states. This number was considerably less than historic levels, and it was a sign of changes brewing in the societal fabric of the world. None of that registered with us, however, as we settled into new routines. Integrating into a college-like, close-knit setting four years earlier than most kids came pretty easily. Possibly this was because many of us came from large families and knew what it was like to live in a community. That's not to say we didn't get homesick, but we found the best way to overcome that was to immerse ourselves in the bundle of activities that were everywhere around us.

Our college prep curriculum was rigorous and kept us continuously challenged. There were no open spots or study halls in the schedule. Consequently our high school course of study included four years of German, Latin, religion, English, math, science, history, and, in my case, glee club. Our instructor for this class was

I am first row, second from right with my arm around Princess

Father Aubert, a gentle-natured priest with an ardent passion for gardening and music. He had a unique talent for taking a restless group of high school boys, some with dubious singing ability, and turning them into a consistently high-scoring group in various competitions around Ohio. The education I received prepared me well for the next step in life. Ohio required twenty credits to graduate high school, but most of us finished with about twenty-seven.

In addition to the educational rigor, another benefit of attending a small school meant we had the opportunity to explore a wide variety of interests beyond the classroom. One year I pursued an interest in radio-controlled aircraft. The Greater Cincinnati Radio Control Club had its home base across the street from school, and the high-pitched sounds of radio-controlled aircraft patrolling the skies filled Sunday afternoons. Their proximity naturally drew my interest, and a number of us delved into it as a hobby. I quickly found however that the few precious minutes of flying had to be supported by hours of work on the airplane, and that reality pushed me into other pursuits. To this day, however, my ear quickly picks up the sound of a radio-controlled aircraft engine, and it takes me immediately back to blue, Ohio skies and Sunday afternoons of many years ago.

St. Francis Seminary

Another mild interest was photography. Tony Schulte, one of my classmates, was one of the primary school photographers. As such he had one of the few student keys to the darkroom. I was fascinated by the photo development process, even though I was not a serious student of photography. Once we started developing pictures, we could not leave the room until the process was complete. I remember some Friday nights developing pictures with Tony and listening to top forty tunes on local WSAI radio. For me the darkroom will forever be synonymous with Joan Baez's "The Night They Drove Old Dixie Down," which always seemed to be playing.

Interests such as student council and writing for the student newspaper kept me occupied, but no other extracurricular activity fueled my passion like sports. We were too small to field a football team, so during the fall we participated in a varsity soccer league. In those days there was no distinction in soccer between large and small schools because the sport was not that well established. That meant we played against some of the city's biggest high schools, including Moeller, Western Hills, Roger Bacon, and others. While we were at a significant size and speed disadvantage, we partially made up for it in reckless aggression. That generally meant we played banged up a lot, but we were reasonably competitive. We also fielded junior varsity and varsity basketball as well as varsity baseball teams. I played all three sports for four years. Even so, I couldn't get enough. To satisfy our physical education requirement with the state of Ohio, we had intramural sports. That allowed me to play fall touch football, winter basketball, and spring softball. I also volunteered as a substitute whenever I could for fall volleyball and winter bowling. A school lake turned winter Saturday afternoons into marathon hockey games. After teaching myself rudimentary skating skills, I joined in the games. I quickly discovered the benefit of being on a team with kids from Michigan or Canada!

Love of sports extended beyond our own playing fields. I followed all the local major league teams, and my favorite was the Cincinnati Reds. Back then they were the "Big Red Machine" and the talk of MLB. I went to their games and the NBA Cincinnati Royals (now the Sacramento Kings) whenever I could. I'll never forget the epic showdown late in the '72–'73 season between "The Big O" Oscar Robertson of the Royals and "Pistol Pete" Maravich of the Atlanta Hawks. It was one of the most exciting NBA games I ever attended. This love of sports fueled a lifelong habit of physical activity and working out. Over time the physical demand of sports such as softball and football gave way to racquetball and basketball and later still to ellipticals, swimming, and bike riding.

THE CATHOLIC EXPERIENCE

High school soccer, I am on bottom row third from left

Hockey picture, I am standing to the right of the goal

Like other high school kids, one of my near single-minded pursuits was food. We usually had one or two extra helpings for every table of seven to eight hungry teenagers, so those interested in the extras would participate in a lottery for the additional servings. Those interested would raise their hands, and someone would spin a knife. Whomever the knife pointed to and the person to his right got the extra helpings. Even though we had universal and generally noncomplimentary nicknames for the food, there was never a shortage of lottery participants. (One such suspicious food was fruit jelly, which had elements of fruit Jell-O in it.) To supplement our seemingly never-ending hunger, school days featured a midmorning snack break called "bun fun." In the context of modern society that term just sounds wrong, but back then it was a highly anticipated daily feature. We would line up by class, and assigned servers would approach with a tray full of baked goods. Typically they were donuts. The server was either a disciplinarian or not. The disciplinarians kept strict order in the process, while those that were not basically tossed the tray at the surging crowd, which caused the process to degenerate quickly.

Whenever I tell someone I attended a high school seminary, one of the first questions is invariably about girls. Being high school boys, we were of course interested in girls, and the most promising opportunity for interaction came through an outreach program on Saturday mornings. That was when our school was paired with McAuley High School (an all-girls Catholic high school) to work with underprivileged kids in Cincinnati's Over-the-Rhine District. One of the oldest and most historic neighborhoods in Cincinnati, it was also severely economically depressed. We picked the age-group of kids whom we worked with, and I always chose middle school. Within a structured setting, our objective was to provide companionship and fun for kids who typically did not have enough of either. Following a morning of activities, we would accompany one of the girls and both of our kids back home. While none of the girls I met remain in my memory today, remembrances of those kids and their living conditions have never left. It was the first time I had come face-to-face with abject poverty, and I sometimes wonder what happened to Lester, the young lad I worked with over several years.

At the end of every academic year, the priests held a school wide meeting. Among other things they encouraged us to enjoy our friends and family back home and to get a job. They told us it was OK to date but admonished us not to "fall in lust." In the end we weren't all that different from millions of other high school boys. We were a lot more talk than action when it came to the opposite sex!

In addition to religion class, we also fostered our vocations through prayer, small group discussions, and attending daily Mass. Additionally St. Francis sat on 183 acres of woods. As when I was growing up, there were times I needed to get away from everyday congestion, and Winton Woods was the perfect place to do that. It was a place of solitude where I could read, think, meditate, and recharge. By the end of my sophomore year, I began to suspect I was not cut out for the priesthood. This was not due to a loss of faith. If anything my faith had been strengthened. I was, however, more aware of the realities of a priestly life, and I began to doubt my calling. By my junior year, I was certain of it, but I did not want to leave St. Francis. I had a special bond with the people and experience I had been part of, and I wanted to finish my senior year there. When I left I did so with a spiritual foundation that is still part of me today. Of our freshman class of twenty-eight, only fourteen graduated, and of those, only one became a priest. It is no wonder high school seminaries ceased to exist in the 1980s.

St. Francis Seminary was a special place, and it attracted special people. Take a look at my freshman class picture. Specifically look at the individual in the back row who is third from the left. That is Ken Salazar, former US senator from Colorado and US secretary of the interior under President Obama. Another individual who enrolled in the 1976–77 academic year was Tom Mapother.... better known today as Tom Cruise! For the rest of us less distinguished individuals who attended or graduated from St. Francis, we left equipped to make the world a better place. We became grounded in our education, our faith, and ourselves.

Tom Mapother, a.k.a. Tom Cruise of Hollywood fame

4

SCHOOL, FAMILY, AND CAREER

In fall of 1973, I had to choose my major as I started college. Like many others at that age, I had no idea what I wanted to do, but I was sure about one thing. I was definitely not going to follow my dad, uncle, and granddad into the heating, ventilating, and air-conditioning (HVAC) business. I didn't have a particular reason other than it just didn't seem very exciting. With that in mind, I decided to enroll as a general education major. By November it was apparent college was just an extension of high school but with several notable differences. First there were a lot more girls in these classes, and second the responsibility for attending class was up to me. A major portion of my grade in history class came from a book research project, and to my surprise and delight, one of my uncle's books was on the approved list. His Book Entitled *Gold Fever* is still available today. My Uncle George earned a Bronze Star in World War II, having served in the 101st Airborne Division. He also earned a Purple Heart in the Netherlands at Arnhem, a battle later memorialized in the movie *A Bridge Too Far*. Interested in writing, he was a correspondent for *Yank Magazine* and wrote an article about the D-day invasion. It was from his perspective offshore Normandy as he waited his turn to wade ashore. Following the war he received a journalism degree at the University of Missouri and moved to New York City with my Aunt Lynn. There they both had writing careers. My aunt wrote children's books, while George wrote historical novels as well as for the American Medical Association. Liberal mentions of my uncle in the final report helped me get an A, and it also gave me the luxury of occasionally bypassing this first period class in favor of card games in the student union. For the most part, however, my first semester of college was more English, more math, and more of the same. Some soul-searching and research led me to change my major to business at the end of the semester.

George Groh and Sons calendar, business started by my grandfather in 1918 and still operating in Emporia Kansas

Eighteen months later and fifteen hours short of my associate degree, I made one of the dumbest decisions I have ever made, though it ultimately proved to have an influential impact on my life. I decided to quit school to begin working full-time at a steel fabrication plant. During the next year, I worked with a number of individuals who told me their life plans when they were nineteen, but then wives and children redirected their pursuits into factory jobs. I came face-to-face with the realization that this future would tether me to a boring, mind-numbing job. The following summer my brother worked in the plant to earn college money, and that spurred our sibling rivalry in a new direction. We both worked a water-cooled welder, which attached barn door rails together. We would compete for the most linear footage completed in an eight-hour day. We approached but never broke three thousand feet. Operating at that speed meant welding a section every two minutes, including water-cooled welder tip maintenance. Running the hollow tip too long chanced a water leak, which was something the foreman seriously frowned on. Other than occasional water leaks however, I was generally in good graces with the foreman. Then he got a call from a farmer in Iowa. Apparently one of his barn doors had fallen off a section of rail that I had welded. The subsequent investigation put a stop to our daily contests, and my brother was reassigned to a large punch press. Late in the summer, with only a few weeks before the start of school, Tom was operating the press without guards. This was standard operating procedure for the plant. The press came down on my brother's hand, cutting off the ring finger of his left hand. That was the first time I came face-to-face with the dangers of industrial accidents. Several months later I was assigned to a two-man crew in another part of the plant. Our job was to unload an eighteen-wheeler's load of steel coil. The job typically took a crew eight hours to unload, but we would usually complete the task by noon. Feigning disapproval, the foreman would take us aside and tell us he did not want to see our faces again until the next morning. I had always been taught to tackle every task with zeal, and I found it wrong to turn a five-hour task into eight because that was the norm. We valued the extra paid time off more than the foreman's disapproval, so our behavior didn't change. The following summer, working on the same large press that injured my brother, I broke my foot when a three thousand five hundred-pound cartload of steel components tipped over. That proved the end of my factory career.

About eight weeks later, I did what I vowed I would never do. I went to work for Fritz Plumbing and Heating, a nonunion contractor in the small town of Walnut, Illinois. Working summers for my Dad's union heating and cooling contracting business, I was not allowed to perform sheet metal or HVAC service work. For the next year, I began to learn the trade and the fact that my mechanical skills would not win any awards. We installed plumbing and heating equipment in new and existing homes, and I apologize to any Walnut residents whose homes were graced by my lack of skill! One such example. In those days copper was used for water lines, and that meant using a star bit to drill a hole into every joist in order to run the line the length of the basement. Sporting my longer hair as was the fashion, it got caught in the drill bit, literally wrapping me around its axis. I could not get untangled, so I called for assistance from my partner, Bill Lind. Instead of coming to my immediate rescue, he called for nearby workers to witness my predicament. Needless to say, that incident and others like it followed me around for a while. One time I was on a different jobsite, and an electrician asked me, "Are you the guy who got his hair stuck in the drill?" There are other such stories, but they will have to stay sealed in my memory!

In 1975 I learned there was more to the industry than being a mechanic. My dad's company underwrote the cost for me to attend a weeklong Job Related Training course hosted by Lennox Industries at their headquarters in Marshalltown, Iowa. That was the first time I met John LaPlant, one of the Lennox instructors. The first class I took involved the basics of electricity, combustion, and refrigeration. I found the technical side very appealing, and John's teaching style always kept things interesting. It's hard to forget his demonstration about the dangers of continuing to push the burner reset button on oil-fired furnaces. The magnitude of the resulting explosion is directly correlated to the number of pushes on the reset button!

Working in a small town for a small company is a unique experience. Some mornings I would meet my crewmate, Bill Lind, at the local cemetery, where he earned side money by using the company backhoe to dig graves. The mid-'70s were not a robust economic time in the Midwest, and a year after I started, work was becoming thin. Fortunately I had signed up a year earlier for the sheet metal workers' union, and my name came up for consideration about the time work ran out at Fritz.

My new employer was Reliable Fabrications of Rochelle, Illinois, a union sheet metal contractor. They were primarily engaged in the installation of heating and cooling systems in residential new construction. I moved to nearby DeKalb, Illinois, home to Northern Illinois University. Two of my siblings, Mary and Tom, were students there. While my days were spent working, all my social contacts were students at the university. As they talked about their classes and plans for the future, I began thinking about my own. This proved to be the seed of my discontent, and I began to yearn for an education leading to a professional sales position.

Working for a union firm meant mandatory evening training classes in nearby Rockford, Illinois. At these classes I learned how to make sheet metal fittings first on paper and then on metal. My paper patterns were perfect, but the metal ones were far from it. Union pay was better, which was good for me but not so good for the union. The higher wage scale made union contractors uncompetitive with nonunion contractors in residential work. Therefore union workers utilized time-saving tools and methods. In the past, when roughing out holes for floor diffusers, we had always used Sawzalls. While effective this process could be slow, and without care a saw blade could break off, the changing of which necessitated additional time. At Reliable I was given a small, electric chain saw for this task. That sped up things considerably, but it had unintended consequences such as cutting into load-bearing joists beneath poorly placed markings for a floor diffuser. That earned me a day off without pay. One year later work once again became thin, so I was looking for new horizons. It seemed like if you live in Illinois long enough, all roads eventually led to Chicago. The Lennox Industries Chicago branch was looking for an inside sales trainee, and, with help from my dad, I landed the position that cemented my career in the HVAC industry.

In 1977 I began what would be a twenty-one-year career with Lennox. The excitement of moving to the Chicago area was tempered by the reality of its cost. Inside sales trainees were paid more in future opportunities than in paychecks, and the paychecks I did get were insufficient to live on. Knowing I would need nicer clothes and suits once I moved to outside sales, I found a part-time evening and weekend job at a men's clothing store at Woodfield Mall in nearby Schaumburg. That job supplemented my income into a barely livable wage. I also learned about men's workplace fashions, and the store provided a steady pool of dating opportunities. Over the next twenty months, I was educated in the sales and technical side of the HVAC business, and I finally felt I had found my calling. Between the two jobs, however, a workweek sometimes stretched to twenty-one straight days. Even working that much, I still led an economically tenuous life. My days in DeKalb fueled a growing passion for finishing college, as I knew it would be critical to my future success in the industry. In 1979 that opportunity presented itself in the form of a promotion to outside sales. Not only did my pay increase significantly, but I also had a company car. This allowed me to quit my part-time job at the men's clothing store and focus once again on my education. That fall I finished the requirements for my

Me and Dave Lennox

associate degree and began research on a school that would allow me to earn a bachelor's degree by attending night classes.

The year 1980 started off in horrible fashion. My younger sister Theresa was killed in an auto accident on a wintry road in January. She was on a rural, two-lane highway and lost control on an icy patch. The news hadn't settled in yet when my dad called the next day to let me know his dad, the Groh family patriarch, had passed away after a long battle with cancer. Within two days we had lost as many close family relatives. It seemed incomprehensible. I had seen my sister and talked with my granddad only a few weeks earlier at Christmas. The family took a daylong drive to the Groh family homestead in Emporia, Kansas. This was followed by a couple days I will never forget. There was a shared visitation, and the next day we attended two funerals. Theresa was the first sibling whose funeral I had to attend. On the same day, we buried a nineteen-year-old and an eight-five-year-old, and it caused me to think about the importance of living a purposeful life. I realized it could all change at any moment.

During the winter semester, I decided to take a coed volleyball class, thinking it would be a fun way to meet girls. I didn't meet any I wanted to date, but I did meet Jim Neidhart, a very outgoing guy who was also a sports enthusiast. He introduced me to sixteen-inch softball, a game played in Chicago without gloves. Wikipedia says this game is sometimes called mush ball, but that term is misleading. While the ball is not as hard as a traditional baseball, doctors in various emergency rooms over the next few years told me the number one cause of broken fingers in Chicago between May and September was sixteen-inch softball. Jim and I started up a team the summer of 1980 in the Chicago Park District league. Unable to find a sponsoring bar that first season, we self-funded a team and called ourselves the Free Agents.

One Saturday morning in late summer, one of my contractors asked me to stop by his shop regarding a project we were working on. When I arrived I found him in the back of the shop where he had a litter of kittens he was seeking homes for. I'm still not sure why, but I said I would take one. Picking a pretty, frisky, gray, long-haired female, I imaginatively named her Kitty, and she was with me for the next twenty-two years. Later that evening I went with my brother Tom to one of our favorite nightclubs in the Near North Side. Gaffers was a fun place that played '50s and '60s music, and the right song would prompt a snake dance that proceeded outside onto Broadway Street. This would bring traffic to a halt, but drivers didn't seem to mind. I liked that the people there were well-educated and had their acts together. That evening I met a girl who forever changed my life, but she didn't make it easy.

When I first approached the blonde girl, who was standing next to a friend, I asked her to dance. She declined. Not willing to accept that for an answer, I asked her what better things she had to do, at which point she accepted. We continued talking and dancing, and at the end of the evening, when I asked for her number, she gave me a folded piece of paper. When I glanced at it, I saw her first name and her company's main switchboard number. When I looked up to ask for more information, she had vanished. Months later, she told me that if I was truly interested and had been listening to our conversation that evening, I would find her. I was and I had been, so the chase was on. A few days later, I called the number, and I was a bit dismayed to find there were a number of Susans at that company. I had to talk to several before I finally found Susan Larson, but the conversations leading up to that ranged from awkward to hilarious. One lady hung up on me, and another volunteered to help me with my search, which I politely declined.

My first date with Sue was to Chicago Fest, a celebration of food and music at Navy Pier. This was when the city was trying to find a good use for the historic pier, and the event featured foods from around the world. Music stages ranged from blues to jazz to country to rock and roll. City bumpkins, neither of us had been exposed to such a variety of food or music. Combined with perfect summer weather, the magnificent skyline in front of us, and Lake Michigan behind us, it made for a memorable day. After dinner we made our way to the Rock on the Roof stage to listen to a performance by Chuck Berry. Conversation with Sue came easily, and we talked long after the final performance of the night. At one point a Chicago cop sternly asked us what the heck we were doing. (He didn't say heck.) He informed us Navy Pier was closed, and we had to get out immediately. Thinking his reaction was a little harsh, I asked him with some irritation what time it was. I figured it was about ten or so, but he curtly informed us it was after one a.m. The day had flown by.

In the fall of 1980, I began a four-year journey as an outside sales rep for Lennox during the day and a part-time marketing and business student at night. I dived into school with a burning desire I had never felt before. I studied not because I had to or because I was afraid of getting a bad grade. I studied because I *wanted* to. That had never been true in the past. I preferred DePaul University for my bachelor's degree, but that school didn't offer a complete assortment of required courses at night. In those days there was no online learning, and most schools catered to day students. Northeastern Illinois University offered a full slate of night classes and state school tuition. Located on the northwest side of the city, it was also in reasonable proximity to where I lived. I felt like all the stars were beginning to align.

Sue and I continued to see each other, settling into a routine of alternate apartment weekends. I lived in the north side and she in the south side, which provided a great opportunity to explore many neighborhoods within the city. In the summer and fall of 1981, I made two decisions that neither of us would ever forget. In the single person's game of revolving apartments, I moved to another North Side apartment. It overlooked Six Corners (Milwaukee Avenue, Cicero Avenue, and Irving Park Road). The apartment was on the fourth floor in an old building with steam heat. The view was great from the bedroom windows. We could watch people perusing the shops of six corners out one window and look over a serene neighborhood park out the other. Kitty never seemed to get tired of it. The winter of 1981–82 was particularly brutal, and it seemed to snow the most on days I chose to stock up at the grocery store and could not find a parking spot closer than a block away. One Sunday stood out above all others that winter. It was early January, the NFL play-offs were on, and Sue came over to the apartment. It just so happened it was the coldest day in Chicago history to that point. It was twenty-six degrees below zero (actual air temp) and seventy-two degrees below zero with wind chill. I had to go for a walk outside just to see what that was like, and Sue thought I was completely insane. Meanwhile the ancient steam boilers in the basement were hopelessly overwhelmed by the demand, and those of us on the fourth floor had it the worst. We could see our breath in my apartment, and Sue wore her coat, hat, and mittens the whole time she was there.

I made the second, much better decision that fall. I proposed to Sue. She said yes, and we set a wedding date for the following August. We decided for a variety of reasons to get married at First Congregational Church of Moline, Illinois, which was Sue's childhood Protestant church. My life experiences after high school had put me at odds with some of the teachings of the Catholic Church. Certain doctrine within the church either didn't make sense to me or I disagreed with them, and I found the application of doctrine to be unevenly applied. I knew getting married in that church was going to be a major issue for my parents, and I anticipated a reaction similar to the one Martin Luther got after posting his ninety-five theses. My parents and grandparents were not far removed from the Protestant and Catholic struggles carried over from Europe. My paternal grandfather was raised Lutheran, and when he told his mother he was marrying a Catholic, she disowned him. Consequently she didn't speak to him again until her deathbed. While not reacting that severely, my parents did express strong, negative feelings about my decision. Perhaps because of my years at the seminary, I felt solid in my convictions, and I believed my parents would someday be at peace with my decision. In the end I can't really see God being all that concerned with whether one is Protestant or Catholic. If a person believes in God, we are all by extension children of God. Why wouldn't he welcome one of his own who had lived out a life of faith, regardless of the denomination or creed followed? Years later my parents' thinking, especially my mom's, did evolve. They even became more comfortable attending the occasional service in a Protestant church when they visited us, and we would always attend Catholic Mass when visiting them.

The next several years flew by. I loved what I was doing in outside sales with Lennox, we had a good group that seemed to run on all cylinders. The customers showed their approval with increasing sales numbers every year. The classes I was taking to complete my degree at Northeastern Illinois University also fueled my adrenaline. I continued to play softball (and break fingers), but the team was becoming less and less mine because of the relentless demand of work and school. I moved into Sue's south side apartment when we got married, so I was no longer close to the neighborhood ball fields. Nevertheless, thirty years later and eight hundred miles distant, I still keep in touch with some of the inaugural team's players.

1985 was a magical year. In December of '84, I graduated with highest honors from Northeastern, and the following July Sue and I bought our first house. It was located in the western Chicago suburb of Elmhurst, a great little community with perfect access to all parts of the city and suburbs. That fall the Bears lost only one regular-season game en route to their Super Bowl championship. That fall also saw the arrival of our firstborn, Stephen James. We hosted a Super Bowl party in January, and at one point I handed Stephen to my friend Jim Neidhart, who was still decidedly single. I am not much of a fisherman, but he definitely had a fish out of water expression.

I decided to continue the momentum of my education by pursuing an MBA at Loyola University of Chicago, and in 1987 Lennox asked me to come to Dallas to interview for a national account sales position. It was a cold February day when I pulled into O'Hare around six a.m. for my flight to Dallas. The electronic sign over the roadway said it was ten degrees, and the early morning hour made it feel colder than that. It was my first trip to Dallas and the first time I had ever visited somewhere warm in the middle of winter. The day was a blur of conversation and interviews, but I remember grabbing a soft drink between meetings. I looked down from the tenth floor onto a condo development next to the headquarters building. A couple was playing tennis in shorts. It was seventy-four degrees that afternoon, and I reveled in the thermal shock. The rest of the day continued in a rush, and all too soon I was flying back to Chicago. As I was leaving the airport around ten p.m., I drove underneath the same electronic sign over the roadway. It once again

Stephen and I on a bicycle in Elmhurst, Ill. in 1987

said the temperature was ten degrees. I couldn't get the thought of the couple playing tennis in shorts only a few hours earlier out of my mind. Somehow I knew I had crossed a Rubicon.

I decided not to accept the national account sales position, but the experience helped me get onto the radar for future promotion. The following year proved decisive in several ways. First Lennox invited me to join a select, nationwide group who would work with contractors in a business and marketing consulting role. There was no precedent for this position in the company or industry, so a lot of eyes would be watching us. It blended perfectly with my nearly fifteen years of industry experience and business degree in marketing. There was no template for the position. Rather we shared experiences across a broad, national platform for feedback. After being in sales for ten years, I was ready and excited for the new opportunity. All this paled, however, next to the other major event that year—the birth of our second son, Eric Joseph. Eric was baptized by Reverend Richard Nye in the same church he had baptized Stephen. He was also Sue's minister growing up and the man who had married us. We quickly found the transition from one child to two a much bigger step than from zero to one, but we truly felt like a family as opposed to a couple with a child. We had talked about the merits and costs of Sue quitting work to become a full-time mom. I assured her I was fully behind her making that move, but she had not yet come to the same conclusion. Over the next six months, I took Stephen to a nearby babysitter every morning, while Sue picked him up every afternoon. We continued to discuss the stay-at-home model, bothered by suggestions from our babysitter to quit holding Stephen so much. The babysitter didn't want him to be used to being held because she had several other infants she was watching at the same time. One night, not long after going to bed, Sue turned toward me and asked what I thought about her quitting work. Having just nearly fallen asleep, I responded in a rather irritated fashion. "You know how I feel. I am fully behind your decision. Now good night." "Good," she said. "I'm going to give them notice tomorrow." With that Sue turned back on her side and fell promptly to sleep. Now I was wide-awake. A million questions flooded my brain. I mentally recalculated our budget from every conceivable angle, but I finally fell asleep with the realization that Sue's decision gave us the best chance to be fully focused on job one, which was trying to be good parents. At the time society devalued and even looked down on women who made these decisions, but we felt it was right for us. We were also truly fortunate that my escalating career allowed us the luxury of making that decision.

Each year seemed to move faster than the year before. I began to travel nationally with the new position, which was something I had not done before. I was also working with the largest customers in Illinois and Indiana, which provided its share of excitement and vexation. The combination of a larger family, travel, greater responsibility, and graduate school was getting increasingly difficult to juggle. Flying back one Friday afternoon from a weeklong industry event in New Orleans, I wasn't looking forward to my arrival at O'Hare. Upon arrival, I would have to make a mad dash to Loyola's downtown campus for a calculus final I knew I was not ready for. Instead of studying I spent most of the flight looking out the window and contemplating. I came to the realization I did not want to admit. School had to go. I felt both guilt and relief in making the decision, but it was the right one. It was fortuitous because Lennox soon approached us about moving to division headquarters in Columbus, Ohio. I would be responsible for one of the elements of the newly created marketing services department. While Sue and I had talked theoretically about such a move, it was different once the discussion turned real. We would be leaving our family, friends, and home. In the end, however, it felt right, so Sue and I embarked on our new adventure. We packed the kids, household goods, and Kitty, and we headed for the land of the Buckeyes.

5

THE ALLIED VAN LINE YEARS

It seemed as if we announced a move in our Christmas letter just about every other year. The first stop was Columbus, Ohio. I was part of the group that started up a marketing department responsible for training and marketing services, consulting services, advertising, and parts center stores. The division marketing manager, Dick Ansley, was one of the most creative people I had ever met. His ideas were so plentiful that you just couldn't keep up with them all. Collectively, however, we successfully implemented many of these ideas and quickly became the best marketing group within Lennox. On the personal side, Ohio State football was *HUGE* and we couldn't help but get swept up in some of the mania. We quickly made friends with another family on our block who had kids of similar age, and from that flowed playgroups for the kids and other activities for Sue.

Two years later Dick had a serious and very unfortunate health setback, and I was named division marketing manager. I was excited about what our group could accomplish together, but that all changed with a phone call one morning. The call was from my boss, the VP and division's general manager. He asked me what I was doing Thursday afternoon. As usual I had more planned than I would likely accomplish, but the nature of this question and the tone in his voice opened the calendar. He asked me to attend a meeting at the airport with some individuals I would recognize when I got there. I was not to tell anyone about the meeting, but he said everything would be clearer afterward. Naturally that conversation drove me nuts over the next few days, and I tried to brainstorm every possibility of what it might be about. No scenario I envisioned was remotely close. The news was staggering. All the division operations were closing, and their functions were being integrated into operations at the Dallas world headquarters. There were about seven divisions throughout the United States and Canada, so thousands of people would be affected. Immediately following this news, I was offered a position as corporate head of business consulting where I would be working for Vicki LaPlant. The only reason I didn't say yes immediately was that I obviously had to talk with Sue and the boys, but I knew their reaction would be the same as mine. The next few months were like a tornado as we prepared to move. The Columbus marketing department worked to hand off responsibilities to new and uncertain groups at corporate. Those of us moving simultaneously assumed responsibilities from divisional counterparts across North America. It was difficult for many as it became apparent who was and wasn't moving to Dallas. It remains one of the most unique work experiences in my career.

Sue and I were excited to move to the sunny plains of Texas. We had lived all our lives in the north with its long, cold, dreary winters. Many of the relocated employees moved to the growing city of Plano, which offered friendly neighborhoods and great schools. We found a ranch home in Plano with a pool about two blocks from an elementary school and park. One of our new neighbors, Karen Secor, brought over cupcakes on our third day, and we quickly made friends. She and her husband, Mike, were hugely supportive

THE ALLIED VAN LINE YEARS

seventeen years later following my accident. Through them we met several other families with kids the same age and in the same school as ours. Over the years Mike and I coached our kids' soccer, T-ball, and basketball teams. With the Jones, Tatum, and Mahoney families, we went camping as part of the Indian Guides organization, and we attended our kids' school activities together. Wealthy, growing areas in DFW, such as Plano, meant our children had unprecedented opportunities for quality educational and life experiences. Collectively our kids were part of Indian Guides, Indian Princesses, Boy Scouts, the school band, school football, school basketball, Odyssey of the Mind, church youth group, swim team, and many other formative groups. Our only rule for our kids was that if you started something, he or she had to finish what they had committed to. We worried a bit, however, that being raised in such a bubble would lead to a skewed worldview.

The neighborhood held a fall pig roast. "Pig Fest," as we called it, was a favorite for all of us. As Pig Fest 1992 arrived, so did our daughter, Christie. She was born that morning about nine a.m., and after spending the day with Sue, I went home. My brother George had been staying with the boys, and the four of us celebrated Pig Fest. It was a fitting end to a wonderful day.

The next few years were tumultuous as Lennox prepared to become a public company. Two years after Christie was born, the marketing department was dissolved as part of a reorganization orchestrated by Andersen Consulting. I was assigned to an Andersen team whose purpose was to turn the Toronto manufacturing plant around. It was interesting and engaging work that succeeded in its purpose, but I knew it was a temporary assignment and I did not know what would come next. It didn't take long to find out however. An outflow of my work with Andersen led to an offer to become the director of a new corporate department called pricing services. For the next year, I worked hard to help our districts become more competitive and more profitable overall. All the while I sensed this too was a temporary assignment. At the end of that year, I took an opportunity to become part of the sales community again as assistant regional manager for the Eastern United States. It was an interesting position, as sometimes I would find myself collaborating with the districts to influence corporate and vice versa. I might go into a district office one day and be heartily welcomed, only to go into another district office the very next day and be hardly welcomed. The travel was pretty constant. I would sometimes wake up in a hotel room, and it would take a few minutes to remember what city I was in. One opportunity we uncovered was in the Mid-Atlantic District. Headquartered in Baltimore its responsibilities included everything down through the Carolinas. The Carolinas represented a growth opportunity, and the customers there didn't particularly appreciate having their district office in Baltimore. There was discussion about creating a separate Carolina district, and Lennox approached me about heading it up. At the time we had an office in Greensboro and a warehouse in Columbia, while the high growth area of Charlotte was being ignored. I proposed we close both offices and open a new, central facility in Charlotte. Lennox agreed, so my family and I prepared to move there in the winter of 1995.

We found the Carolinas to be a tremendous paradox both personally and professionally. We quickly built a great team in Charlotte and set about working to grow our presence. The Carolinas were a form of paradise. In a day's drive, we could traverse from the mountains in Asheville to the seashore at Kitty Hawk. For a history buff like me, I couldn't ask for a better location. History even touched professional sports teams. The Charlotte Hornets NBA basketball team was so named because during the Revolutionary War, Tory sympathizers wrote back to England that the Carolinas were a "hornet's nest" of rebel activity. Winter was minimal, and spring brought a virtual explosion in color, more so than anywhere I had ever seen.

Ribbon-cutting for new Lennox Charlotte facility August 1996. I am in the middle with tie, cutting the ribbon

During our short time there, we took advantage of as much sightseeing as possible. We took vacations to visit Kitty Hawk, Charleston, Asheville, and the Appalachian Mountain countryside. Through Boy Scouts Stephen and I camped at historic Kings Mountain. As a family we also explored the city sites in Charlotte and Raleigh. It felt as if we were living in vacation country. The culture was also steeped in tradition, and, as one veteran from the Southeast told me, "You will either like it or you won't, but there is no in-between." The Charlotte-Mecklenburg School District was still operating under a twenty-five-year-old Supreme Court desegregation order, and consequently kids in the neighborhood went to a disparate collection of schools. An unintended consequence was that neighborhood parents didn't have much in common, so the sense of community was severely compromised.

A year and a half later, we decided to leave Charlotte, despite loving the area, my work, and the people with whom I worked. We targeted both Chicago and Dallas, not knowing at the same time Lennox was targeting us.

In the fall of 1996, we took the trip of a lifetime, a Lennox incentive trip to Germany. Everything about that trip was superlative. We stayed at the Four Seasons in Munich and saw all that delightful city's requisite sites. I was eager to use the four years of German I had forgotten from high school and found a perfect opportunity. Early every morning farmers would set up a market in the Marienplatz under the shadow of the Rathaus-Glockenspiel. Each day I would get up about an hour before Sue and walk the short distance to the market, where I stopped at a particular pastry vendor. He knew I was an American who did not want to speak English, and he seemed to delight in helping me speak German. Every morning I would allow him to suggest a new pastry as we carried on a halting conversation. It was a very energizing way to start the day.

One day Sue and I struck out on our own in a rental car to get closer to the Alps in Oberammergau. My parents had been there twenty-five years before and had brought me back a souvenir beer stein. I found the exact same beer stein and purchased it for both my parents and ourselves. The twin steins still sit on our fireplace mantel. We also drove on the autobahn, which is an experience everyone should have. My only regret was I did not get a car with enough horsepower, so we could only do about one hundred miles per hour. It sounds crazy, but that is not fast enough to pass safely on that roadway. Another day we took a group tour to Neuschwanstein Castle, which is the one depicted in numerous Disney ventures. On the way our bus took a break in a small town, parking near the town square. I wandered over to look at the statue of soldiers, which dominated the square. It was a monument to German soldiers from the area who had died in World War II. On the one hand, I understood the monument's humanity. On the other hand, it seemed almost wrong. To see wrong front and center however was to visit the Dachau concentration camp. As soon as we walked into the main building, we were greeted with multiple, large, glass-enclosed displays of shoes from people who had perished in the camp. It was sobering and disturbing.

During our trip I was approached about taking over the Chicago district. Some weeks later we agreed, and we began the process of moving back to the Windy City. It seemed to make sense. My parents were in Peoria, and my brother was in Chicago. Sue's father passed away in 1995, but her mom and twin sister, Nancy, were in the nearby Quad Cities (Moline, Illinois, Davenport, Iowa, Rock Island, Illinois, and Bettendorf, Iowa). By March 1997 we were back in Elmhurst, about a half mile from the first house we had ever purchased. The kids settled in well, and we felt we had made the right decision. By the end of the year, my parents retired to a small town outside Springfield, Missouri, and Nancy's family relocated to, of all places, Plano, Texas. Nevertheless we regularly got together with Sue's mom and my brother. The work continued at a torrid pace, but one year after our move, I decided to move in a different direction after twenty-one years with Lennox. It was not a move I made lightly, but it was the right one.

For the next two years, I was the marketing director for Excelsior Manufacturing and Supply, a Chicago-based sheet metal manufacturer and distributor with operations in Missouri, Kansas, Indiana, and Minnesota. In 1999 Sue's mother passed away just before Christmas, and there didn't seem to be much holding us to the Chicago area anymore. Stephen would be entering high school in the fall, and we knew it was critical for our kids to have a stable high school experience. My thoughts and résumés kept going to Texas, but the first opportunities came in Chicago and Detroit. I explored these opportunities in detail but was not interested. I also met with some trusted Lennox friends to analyze an ownership opportunity in Cincinnati with an appliance parts distributor. I was not excited about this organization, however, and during the flight back to Chicago, I wondered what the new century would bring. Within a few months, the Texas prodding began yielding results. The Trane Company wanted me to interview for a position in Tyler, and Titus wanted to interview for a position in Richardson. I made four trips to Texas in a fairly short time frame. The Trane opportunity looked like an extension of everything I had done with Lennox, while the Titus opportunity, as Robert Frost wrote, was the road less traveled by. The choice was clear. A new direction was in order.

Even though I felt I was changing career paths at forty-five, the decision to work for Titus turned out to be one of the best decisions I ever made. I wasn't so sure at first, though. On the first Monday of every month, we had a major projects meeting, which was a detailed review of our product development projects with manufacturing and senior management. It was not a meeting to come unprepared for. This meeting was coming up one week after I started, so David (Titus VP and my boss) called Jenny Abney (VAV product manager), Terry Kelley (VAV design engineering manager), and me into his office for a review. I left that meeting wondering if I had made the right decision. Even after twenty-five years in the business, I pretty much had no idea what they were talking about. Over time, however, everything made a lot more sense. Titus had plenty of engineers for the design, testing, and development work. My task was to ensure everything coalesced into dollars and sense in the form of new products for our customers.

On the personal side, the move to Texas could not have gone smoother. We found a house within a half mile of where we lived before, and once again we were across the street from our friends the Secors. Now the kids were back in the same school they had left only five years earlier. The only difference was Eric had been bumped up one grade in the Carolinas. Sue reconnected with old friends, and the company for whom she worked in Chicago had an opening for the same position in the DFW area. That enabled her to go back to work part-time at a job she was familiar with in the Plano area where we lived. I was working only a few miles from the Lennox corporate facility and knew the area well. It was the smoothest transition we had ever made.

When we moved back to Texas, Stephen was going into ninth grade. When school started, he asked if he could go out for the football team. Football runs nearly as deep in Texas as oil, but we had mixed feelings. We realized it was important to him, however, so we agreed. Eric also had the bug and went out for his seventh grade team. That began six years of *Friday night lights* for us. Sue and I would divide and conquer. One went to Stephen's game and the other to Eric's. The experience was over all too quickly, and I still remember Stephen's senior night when they announced his name as he ran through the tunnel of cheerleaders and onto the field for the last time. I had a lump in my throat, and the process was duplicated two short years later with Eric. Meanwhile Christie was drawn to volleyball and basketball. She started playing competitive basketball in second grade, so many Saturday or Sunday afternoons were spent traveling to various gymnasiums in the DFW area. Sue and I thoroughly enjoyed all their events and rarely missed any of them.

At Titus changes were in the works in 2006. David had accepted a promotion to president of ASC (Titus's parent company), and his replacement interestingly came from the Charlotte district office I had opened at Lennox. At about the same time, a headhunter contacted me about a significant opportunity—vice president of sales and marketing for PCI, Inc., in Fort Worth. I did not know much about them other than that they manufactured louvers, dampers, and acoustical and architectural products. The opportunity was very intriguing. Conversations continued for several months, and then I accepted their eventual offer. Stephen was a junior at Texas A&M University—Commerce, and Eric was starting his freshman year at Abilene Christian University on a football scholarship.

Christie was starting her freshman year of high school, and that was a concern because PCI wanted me to move closer to Fort Worth. We talked with Christie, and she was OK with the move despite some trepidation. We all agreed the timing would be better at the end of Christie's freshman basketball season, which was the spring of 2007. When the time came, we purchased a home in Grapevine in the Southlake School District.

Meanwhile at PCI I once again faced a product knowledge hurdle. I was expected to learn the technical side of the product, which I eagerly undertook. Spending many hours at night, I studied product performance and application. Our focus on the sales side of the organization was expanding our markets and bringing in additional technical support staff. We also brought to life an initiative called PCI Technical Institute. Initial rollout of the institute offered two-day classes for our reps in the principles of louvers and dampers, architectural products, and acoustics. They were extremely well received. By the spring of 2008, things seem to be firing on all cylinders. Stephen had just graduated from college with a degree in construction science and was going to work for a Chicago-based general contractor. Eric had just finished his sophomore year at ACU and was majoring in marketing. He planned to stay in Abilene over the summer, working at Cracker Barrel and participating in summer workouts with the football team. Christie had just completed her sophomore year of high school and was seeing some playing time on a talented Southlake Carroll basketball team that made the state play-offs. Sue continued her employment with a Plano-based Farmers Insurance agency, working from home three days and commuting to the office the other two. Sue and I were still getting used to not having the boys at home, and we were looking forward to the upcoming Father's Day weekend so we could spend some time with them.

6

JUNE 15, 2008

Bike trail in Oak Grove Park

Sunday morning, Father's Day was rather hectic. We took Christie to Plano that morning for her youth mission trip, attended church services and headed back to Grapevine for lunch with Stephen. The afternoon was quite the opposite, we relaxed with each other's company and shared the pleasure of doing nothing. By the time Sue was ready to take Stephen to the airport, I was feeling restless. I had not worked out all weekend and decided a bike ride was in order. I wheeled my bike out of the garage into the 100° sunlight, put on my headphones and mounted my bike. I adjusted the radio channel to country station 99.5 "The Wolf." As I started down the driveway I heard the radio announcer proclaimed, "It's five o'clock in Texas."

The next thing I knew, I was lying on the ground, and my head hurt. It was hot, and I felt as if I was in a peculiar position. I realized I had been unconscious, and in my mind the peculiar position was like a dog lying on its back. The feeling was so real I didn't question it. I began to look around at my surroundings, and I was alarmed when I looked down at my left side. My arm was lying flat on the ground, but that was not where it felt like it should be. About that time I realized I could not move.

I could hear the people whom I had seen just a couple of minutes before in their boat, so I began calling out for help. My voice was not as loud and strong as it normally was, and I didn't know why. After a short time, I realized two things. First they were not going to be able to hear me, and second I had to conserve my energy. I began calling for help in an almost chant like fashion, hoping someone on the trail might hear me. That went on for a few minutes. New thoughts began to race through my brain. What if no one heard me or found me, and I was out there all night? I estimated it was about six p.m. And wondered if the dinner hour would empty the trail. As these and other thoughts began to take hold, I tried to yell louder. I quickly realized that was unsustainable. No matter how hard I tried, I could not yell louder. If I continued to yell and panic, I knew I would hyperventilate. I stopped yelling and took stock of my situation. I still did not know why my arms and legs felt as if they were in the air, and I started to focus on the fact that I couldn't move anything. I closed my eyes, cleared my head of all thought and said a prayer that someone would find me soon. The thought of not being able to move should have terrified me, but I never gave serious thought to the fact I might die. I realized, however, I needed to mentally condition myself for the potential of a very different future.

I knew there was a high likelihood I was in serious trouble, and I thought about what that might mean. I consciously thought about the fact that my future would be largely shaped by my attitude, and I did not want that future to be negative. I vowed then and there to never look back, never give up, and remain positive.

The heat was starting to become a problem. My forehead was getting sunburned, and between that and the bump from the fall, I was developing a headache. I was also very thirsty. I started again to rhythmically yell. "Help! Help me please!" I closed my eyes, cleared my mind, and put all my energy into continuing this chant.

After a few moments, I heard a shout back. "Hey, buddy, where are you?" Relief flooded over me. Seconds later a man stood next to me, providing shade from the intense sun. A young girl of about eight stood next to him. I presumed it was his daughter. "What happened," he asked. I told him I had crashed the bike and could not move. The girl had a bottle of grape Gatorade, and the man asked her for it. "Are you thirsty?"

"Yes," I said. He poured some carefully into my mouth, as I could not sit up. To this day that sip of grape Gatorade tops my list of best drinks of all time. After doing it a second time, he told me he was going to look for help, and he would be right back. I found out later he did not have a cell phone, so he went out to a nearby street and flagged down the first car he saw. That driver did have a cell phone and called 911. Before he reappeared I heard a distant siren and felt a second wave of relief. I was only about a mile from the closest firehouse and knew help would be there soon. It was very unsettling hearing that siren and knowing it was coming for me.

I heard the ambulance pull up and stop, but I could not see it. Seconds later two EMTs came through the brush and asked me what hurt. "Not much," I replied. I described the bike crash, how I hit my head, and how I could not move. After checking a few things, they retreated to a spot about ten feet away, and I could tell they were talking with someone via radio. I couldn't help feeling concern when I heard them discuss calling Care Flight. I knew they didn't call Care Flight unless things were serious. They walked back over and told me they were going to put on a neck collar, put me on a stretcher, and put me into the ambulance. My first sensation in the ambulance was the cold temperature, but after lying in the hot sun for however long it felt good. (I later found out I was lying there about forty-five minutes.) They attached various probes that transmitted my vital signs to the hospital. Then one of the EMTs asked if there was someone I wanted to call, and I told him my wife. In reality I didn't want to call because I didn't want Sue to know how badly I was hurt. He asked for the number, and I gave it to him. I told him under no circumstances was he to tell her I couldn't move. He got Sue on the phone and told her I was involved in a bicycle accident, and they were taking me to Parkland. I was continuing to get clues about the situation's seriousness. Normally they would've taken me to Baylor Grapevine, which wasn't far away. Parkland is a level-one regional trauma center and is where JFK was taken after he was shot. I heard her ask the EMT where Parkland was, and I could tell by the conversation her anxiety was rising as she also realized the meaning of going to Parkland. I told the EMT to tell her to take my car with the built-in GPS. Sue told me later that hearing my voice calmly talking to the EMT reassured her. She fortified herself with the belief that my attitude, intelligence, and sense of humor would make all the difference. Even so she dreaded what she would find once she got to Parkland.

The ride to the hospital took about thirty minutes, and I was engaged in conversation with the EMT nearly the whole way. He asked if my left leg hurt. I replied in the negative and asked why. "Apparently you landed in a fire ant bed, and they did a number on you," he said. While that wasn't good, I figured not feeling it was a much bigger problem. When we arrived at the hospital, I was listed in critical condition. They wasted no time getting me into the emergency room, and I was immediately swarmed by doctors and nurses. The ER was very cold because I was only wearing a T-shirt and swimming trunks. They proceeded to cut my clothes off, which didn't help the being cold situation. I was about to discover that spinal cord injuries are like upper-level college classes. They carry prerequisites. One of them is Forget About Your Dignity 101. Even if you object to this treatment, there is nothing you can do about it anyway. On that particular day, however, I had yet to learn that lesson and asked for something to keep me warm. A nurse kindly covered me up.

Sue felt her heart sink as she listened to the EMT tell her what had happened. Sue departed for Parkland immediately, and when she arrived, I greeted her with a smile. Two doctors said something about administering a stick test, whereby they probed me with needles and recorded the results on a sheet of paper. Each time they asked if I could feel anything, and I said no. Perhaps not believing their results, they ran the test a second time. They finished with my feet. I watched them poke me in various places on my foot, and when I told them I could not feel anything, they gave each other a grim look I will never forget.. At that point I was mentally coherent and didn't fully know about my physical situation. The rest of the evening I was shuttled from one place to another for CTs, MRIs, and other tests. When they put me in the MRI machine for a full-body scan, I was very uncomfortable. I was completely enclosed, and my nose was mere inches from the top of the tube. I asked them to put an opaque washcloth over my face. This allowed me to control the situation with my mind. They told me not to move at all, and I didn't bother to tell the darn fools that was why I was in the machine in the first place. I closed my eyes and let my mind flow in rhythm with the machine's sounds. At one point I envisioned myself as a highway worker drilling holes in the concrete at another I was a gunner aboard a navy vessel. On the few occasions I did open my eyes, I couldn't see anything, so I simply went back into my imagination. Since the accident I have gone back to the well of imagination many times, including when I can't go to sleep at night, during certain medical procedures, or other times when I am powerless to control my environment.

While this was going on, Sue began calling the kids. She left a message on Stephen's phone to call her as soon as possible. (Stephen was still in the air on the way to Arizona.) Then she reached Eric, who reacted with shock. "How did it happen," he asked Sue. "He will be fine, right?" Eric looked for reassurance Sue could not provide.

When Stephen landed in Phoenix, he turned on his phone. It started chirping nonstop for about five minutes, so he dialed the mailbox and began listening to his messages. He heard one from Sue and another from Eric. Stephen called Eric first. "They don't know much. There was an accident," Eric said.

"Should I come back," Stephen asked. Eric said he did not know and to call Mom. Stephen called Sue and could tell things were not OK. Sue reassured him it was too early to know anything and that he should keep going. Stephen arrived at his home in Yuma around midnight. All wound up, he could not sleep. At 5:15 a.m. Stephen decided to call his boss to take him back to the airport. All he was focused on was getting back to Texas.

At some point the doctors must have administered anesthetics. I began to feel sleepy and out of it. When they finally wheeled me into my intensive care room, the clock said 11:30 p.m. They told me I was going into surgery the next morning at 6:00 a.m. If they told me why, I don't remember. I didn't realize they had rearranged the hospital operation schedule to put me first on the list.

7

ICU AND RECOVERY

On Monday morning I awoke to the hustle and bustle of various attendants getting ready to move me. We were on our way to the operating room, and I noticed the clock said 6:00 a.m. I had a great view of the ceiling on the way, so I began a game of identifying all the devices I saw. There were a lot of them, and I wondered how many actually worked. At one point we stopped on the first floor, and I had a few minutes with Sue. I honestly didn't know what was going to happen, but I told her I loved her, and if I didn't make it, to communicate the same to the kids. As I was wheeled away, it struck me how alone she looked.

Up early and preparing to drive home, Eric felt angry and depressed. Some people he had confided in the night before had told him things happen for a reason. Eric felt it unjust that something like this could happen to someone who worked so hard for his family, his job, and everything else. It seemed wrong that this could have happened to his dad. Thinking about things happening for a reason, Eric found that line of reasoning to be one of the biggest expressions of BS he had ever heard.

When the office opened at eight a.m., Sue called Pat Cockrum (PCI president and my boss) to tell him what was going on. Despite what had to be a busy Monday, Pat left immediately for Parkland. He was the only one in the waiting room with Sue during my surgery, and we are still grateful for that act of kindness. Sue also called my sister Sue in Illinois to tell her the news. Later my sister told me her mind wouldn't let her believe I would remain paralyzed, but Sue's tone told her this was serious. My sister promptly packed a bag, purchased an airline ticket, and was by my bedside later that day.

Soon we reached the OR, and the presiding doctors introduced themselves with the charm of prison guards. (Not that I really know what they are like.) The silence in the room was too stilted even for a Monday morning at six a.m. I tried to engage the doctor in a conversation about the critical environment diffuser overhead. He brusquely cut me off to tell me the plan. He said something about spinal fusion between C2 and C6 and the installation of a lot of hardware. I didn't understand everything he was talking about, but his tone strongly suggested it was a one-way conversation that wouldn't be repeated. What I took away from his monologue was I had broken my neck and damaged my spinal cord in the vicinity of the C3 or C4 vertebra. Knowing they would put me under soon, I prayed for my survival in the coming operation. I also prayed for God to keep Sue and the kids in his care if I did not survive. I barely finished that prayer when the anesthesiologist knocked me out.

I woke up in the afternoon, and the first thing I noticed was a tube in my throat. I could not talk. During surgery the doctors had performed an endotracheal intubation and connected me to a ventilator. That was a serious inconvenience! We worked out a system whereby I would blink my eyes in code in order to send a message. The message I most often blinked was, "When can they

ICU AND RECOVERY

take this tube out?" My throat was parched beyond description, and they could not give me any relief. What I didn't know then was, if my injury had been an inch or so higher, I would have been like Christopher Reeve, a permanent vent-dependent quad. When I am feeling sorry for myself, I think about how I could be permanently vent-dependent, or I think about those with diseases such as ALS. There are others much worse off than me, and I need to be thankful for what I have. I always knew that, but my present situation made it much easier to truly understand.

When Eric arrived at the hospital, he came through the ER. As he searched for the ICU waiting area, he encountered homeless people asking for money. The sight of critically ill patients coupled with destitute people only deepened his depression. The next few days seemed an endless period of Code Blues and watching body bags being taken from the ICU. When Stephen arrived he found a lot going on. Seeing me for the first time was a shock, but Stephen told me I needed to get better so he could beat me again at racquetball. (It was only the week before Father's Day weekend Stephen had beaten me for the very first time.) The hospital didn't allow many visitors over the next few days. I actually don't remember much about that first week, but I do remember Sue, the kids, Pat Cockrum, and my sister Sue being there. My sister Sue is an optimist, and at one point she told me she was certain I would be up and around in no time. I do not remember that conversation, but one of the ICU nurses took her quietly aside and told her to stop saying that. For Eric the first twenty-four hours comprised the slowest day in his life. It was agonizing, painful, and depressing.

Christie's first day at APPA involved reshingling a roof on a particularly hot Arkansas day. Coming back to the local high school where they were staying, Christie took a shower before dinner. She was walking toward the cafeteria when the youth director, Abe Smith, pulled her aside. Everything she heard was a blur until she talked with her mom. On the other line, Christie could sense Sue was clearly upset as she explained something had happened to Dad. Christie became angry. She had no idea what was going on. Her throat tightened, and tears welled up in her eyes as she digested the news. She felt as if her world was tumbling down, and her legs could not bear her weight. She dropped to the ground, sitting on the grass and trying to understand. Sue explained that Dad was still the same person, and fortunately he had not sustained any brain damage. Sue told Christie she could talk with Dad on Tuesday after they removed the tube from his throat. When Christie hung up, she felt scared and concerned. Her mind filled with a million questions, and she thought back to saying good-bye before she left on her mission trip. Had she given Dad a hug? She could not remember. Had she told Dad she loved him? Had that been the last time she could hug Dad or even see him?. What did she know about paralysis? She began thinking of things she would miss if her dad was a permanent quadriplegic. If it meant they would never play basketball together again, that hurt more than she could explain. She felt she had not taken advantage of the time they had to play together. She wondered if he would be there to walk her down the aisle one day. Thoughts and questions continued to flood her mind for the rest of the night. She didn't know how long she cried while lying on her sleeping bag that evening, but finally sleep took her where reality could not haunt her.

The next day they took the tube out of my throat. I can tell you that was the single worst, nastiest, most horrible, and most awful thing I have ever been through. It was very difficult for Sue to watch as well. When they finally removed it, they still wouldn't give me liquid or even ice chips. I wanted to throttle them but unfortunately couldn't! I had a terrible sore throat for days, and the pleasure of the first few ice chips they gave me rivaled the grape Gatorade I drank right after my injury. That day Christie took her anger out on every nail she pounded into that black roof. The night before my accident, Christie had told a friend that life was good and her faith had never really been tested. Now she felt those words coming back at her like a slap in the face. Later that afternoon she called, and her voice sounded tentative. I knew she was scared, and I sought to reassure her. She said my voice sounded different. She wanted to come home, but I convinced her I was stable. If she came home, I told her there wouldn't be anything she could do to help. I knew if she stayed she would be surrounded by more support than we could provide. She decided to stay, and for the remainder of the week, her friends and adult leaders rallied around her. They talked with her when she wanted and left her alone when she needed. She will never forget their support, even if her behavior didn't show it at the time. During dinner that week, one of her friends was joking about something as she walked over and tickled Christie's neck. Christie had to get up and leave as she realized her dad would never tickle her neck again.

Visitors became more plentiful over the next few days. Even though there was a strict limit on how many could be present and the hours they could be there, the nurses seemed to make an exception for us. As in any business, there are some customers that are more likable than others, and they seemed to take a liking to us. Taking a break one day, Eric stepped outside for a moment. There he saw an unbelievable sight. An elderly, hunchbacked woman in a hospital gown with her IV and oxygen was outside Parkland smoking a cigarette. It felt like just another addition to the depression of his everyday life. As Eric walked through the parking lot to his car one evening, it struck him that regular life was continuing on for most people, but his life had been turned upside down. It seemed so unfair. Every night after leaving the hospital, everyone would go home and research spinal cord injuries. Eric remembers it being like a team of researchers working to cure something. Sleep was hard to come by. On Friday night Christie came home from APPA, and the first sight that greeted her was the flood of flowers and baked goods crowding the living room and kitchen. These were all acts of generosity from friends and neighbors, but she wished we didn't need them. On Saturday Christie visited, and Sue prepared her by letting her know I could not hug her, but she should kiss me on the cheek. When Christie did, she saw the scratches all over my forehead from the crash. Meanwhile Pat came every day, and we began to sort out how to tell reps about my situation. The week after I had been hurt, I was scheduled to make an important trip to Ohio to establish new representation in Cincinnati and Cleveland and meet our Columbus and Toledo reps. I didn't want those opportunities to be delayed, so Pat and I talked about these and other issues. As we talked I realized how powerless I was to physically accomplish anything, and it was unbearably frustrating. I would learn that I had to trust and rely on others, providing patient and coherent guidance with my words. It is a task I continue to struggle with, some days succeeding more than others. I particularly work on patience, since this condition is a difficult pill to swallow for someone who was driven and self-reliant.

After a second week in the ICU, I was moved to a regular patient room for a few days. I was too well for the ICU but not well enough to enter a rehab hospital. We had to make some important decisions over those few days about things we were ill prepared to decide. This included where we were going for rehab and how to handle the financial ramifications of my injury

A regular room at Parkland is to the ICU as a frozen dinner is to Ruth's Chris Steak House. Directly outside my room was the helipad for the hospital's Care Flight operations. Between the unannounced nurse visits at two a.m. and the random but regular comings and goings of the Care Flight helicopter, sleep was hard to come by. Eric and Sue took turns sleeping in my room every night. It was indicative of the support my family would provide, and I very much appreciated it. Sue woke with every distraction, but I don't remember

Eric's sleep being deterred too much by the craziness. Before going to sleep, however, Eric would stare out the window at the tall, green, lit building (the Bank of America Tower) in downtown Dallas and wondered how life was going to change. It was such a bleak moment and one he will always remember. One day without notice aides came to put me in a wheelchair for the first time. It was the first time I had been out of bed since my accident, and I was excited. Often patients who sit up after a long duration of lying down will pass out, but I had no issues. Because of that they let me stay up in the wheelchair a little longer, which I was grateful for.

8

BAYLOR INSTITUTE OF REHABILITATION

The Sues (my wife and sister) and Eric researched rehab hospitals every night at home. While we all talked about four facilities, there was no doubt where we would likely go. Craig in Denver, RIC in Chicago, and TIRR in Houston all were discussed because they were among the country's top rated facilities based on the *US News & World Report*. Not as highly rated but much more convenient (and still listed on the *US News & World Report)* was Baylor Institute for Rehabilitation (BIR) in Dallas. We asked them to send a representative so we could discuss the possibility of me attending. That same day a very good-looking, well-dressed, young woman came by with a slick brochure. She told us every patient was different, but we would typically be there seven to eleven weeks. During that time we would undergo a wide variety of physical, emotional, and informational rehab that would fully prepare us for our new lives. The brochure told us the challenging therapies could take extraordinary patience and will on our part, and the spinal cord injury specialists would encourage us to accomplish everything, and perhaps even more than we imagined, we could. We bought it. A few days later, the ambulance transferred me to BIR to the traumatic brain injury (TBI) floor. The first thing they did was put me in a sling and hoist me off the bed like a baby delivered by a stork. The purpose was to weigh me, but it felt odd and like an affront to my dignity. Over time I learned to get over such affronts because they were never-ending. I was not transferred to the spinal cord floor because I kept running an intermittent fever. My roommates were three others with traumatic brain injuries. One was a young man about Eric's age who had recently incurred his injury in an auto accident. His family was constantly at his bedside, trying to figure out their next steps. Every day Eric looked at him and was thankful for his own life, health, and family. Another was a lady in her thirties or forties who only had one visitor the week I was there. While I certainly was not physically at the top of my game, what I saw on that floor was enough to break my heart. These poor individuals and their families faced a lot more difficult futures than I, and I thought it would do everyone good to spend a week on a floor like this. Finally I was deemed well enough to move to the spinal unit, but I still think of the individuals on the TBI floor and wonder where they are now.

While in ICU we sent a letter to the Grapevine newspaper to discover the name of the individual who found me on the trail. We were hoping to meet and thank him. Somehow two television stations became aware of the story, and one aired a hard news piece about what had happened. They mentioned they were looking for the individual who had helped us. The next day the second station sent out a news crew to interview me and David Clubb, a next-door neighbor who had been exceedingly helpful right after the accident. For a couple of days thereafter, nurses and aides came into my room and said, "Hey, you're that guy they were talking about on TV last night." When the final story aired, however, it contained a lot more drama than we ever intended or expected. The headline was something like, "Grapevine Man is Looking for His Guardian Angel." Eventually it worked out. We did meet the man who found me and his daughter who provided the grape Gatorade I had found so heavenly. Maybe he was my guardian angel after all.

I was looking forward to physical rehab, and I was especially curious how hydrotherapy and transfer therapy worked. Every morning Rodney started my day with physical therapy, and at the end he would pat my leg and tell me to have a blessed day. Following that two strong, silent types would put me in a wheelchair and take me downstairs to occupational therapy. This was the main therapy room where patients were taught how to transfer in and out of beds, cars, chairs, etc. My therapy consisted of arm exercises, but I did not have any other workouts. In the afternoon I would again be taken downstairs to the therapy room for additional occupational therapy.

In the ensuing weeks, we attended classes about caring for spinal cord injuries and assistive technology. One of the more comical devices was a long wooden stick with a rubber tip on the end. It was meant to be strapped to your head and used to turn the pages of books or magazines. It didn't work very well, and we named it the Aardvark. No one ever discussed any other physical therapies, however, and I assumed they would come in the future. After my therapy session, I was taken back upstairs where I spent time in a casual break room across the hall from my room. This is where we conducted our planning sessions about everyone's schedule, questions for the doctor, and needs we would have to address once we left rehab. The room had Wi-Fi access, so we checked e-mail using my old work laptop. Pat had been gracious enough to let us keep it. It was a critical part of my time in rehab, as we used it for both communication and research. We developed questions for our morning meetings with the doctor, and these were dutifully recorded on a whiteboard in my room. The break room was also used by BIR staff, but we generally had a small crowd at all times between the kids, Sue, and various visitors. Vicki and John LaPlant were frequent visitors, they were extremely helpful in planning, research and keeping our morale up. In the early 90s, I had worked for Vicki at Lennox, and I first met John in the mid-'70s when I attended a technical training class at Lennox's corporate facility in Marshalltown, Iowa. By the time I left, we were very familiar (and very tired) of that room.

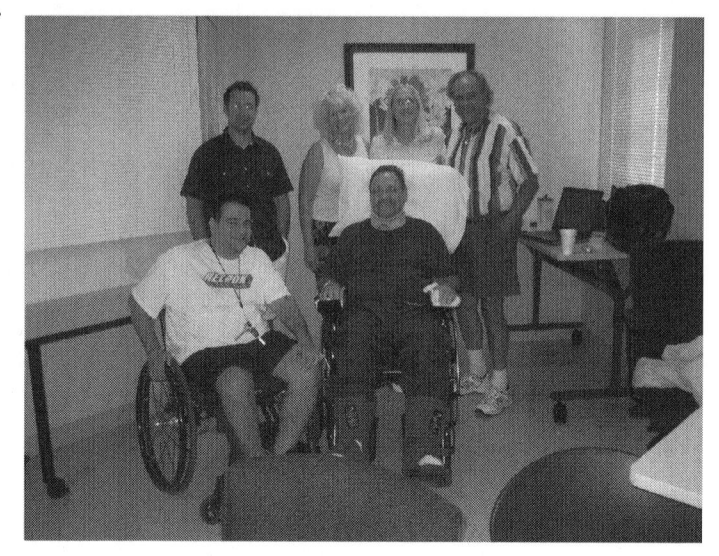

**Baylor rehab, me with another patient.
Back row L to R, Dave Moody, Vicki
Laplant, Sue, John Laplant**

Every Monday morning, Sue and I met all the doctors for a weekly planning update. The doctors sat at a U-shaped table, and we faced them at a table in front. We were excited for our first meeting, and we had brainstormed a long list of questions in anticipation. We walked in with high expectations but sensed something was wrong the minute we entered the room. The doctors all looked grim, and they were not looking at each other or us. That was disconcerting, but Sue took her seat and waited for Dr. Bruce, the program chair, to open the meeting. He looked at Sue and me and started the meeting by telling us we would be at BIR for three weeks. The look of shock was palpable on our faces. We talked about diet, therapies, and other things, but we were still in disbelief. The saleswoman had told Sue and me it would be seven to eleven weeks, and I held out hope some of the therapies might help me gain back some movement.

The announcement about three weeks was like being punched in the gut. My first thought (and the one I still believe) was the doctors did not anticipate me gaining any movement, so they were simply going to continue providing therapy and education about living with a spinal cord injury. We weren't typical patients. If I wasn't going to regain any movement, I would rather have been told that directly. We threw everything we had at tackling this new life. Sue jumped in to assist with my very first shower because she felt she needed to learn these new skills right away. We had been visited by one high-level quad who recommended the spouse not be the primary caregiver. Sue couldn't understand why she would let someone else do that if she were able. She wondered how one could love someone and turn his or her care over to another. Sue's parents had always taught her and her two sisters empathy. Eric was fully involved as well. He did not shy away from tackling any needed procedure. Baylor did, however, overlook caregiver education. My three-week treatment plan was probably a function of my diagnosis and feedback from the insurance company. My insurance was fantastic, and I cannot complain about it, but I think insurance is geared toward keeping people in rehab only as long as they are physically improving. Since I was apparently not expected to improve physically, coverage was only extended for the time it would take for the equipment to be delivered that was covered by insurance. In retrospect it's hard to argue with this rationale, but at the time it was a total surprise. No doctor ever told me I was not expected to recover any movement, and they deftly sidestepped questions of that type. We took our clues from what wasn't said and how our questions were answered. Everything we had been planning went into the trash heap, including the idea of selling our house and looking for something more appropriate. An underlying, gnawing, urgent fear replaced those plans, as we realized we were going back to a home I couldn't even get into.

These were the worst times for Sue. She felt very alone, praying we would find a way through this. From the very first, she knew everyone needed to be strong. Wishing we could turn back time was futile. She didn't believe this accident was God's will; it was simply a freak accident. Sometimes the implications of my injury would hit her like a bolt from the blue, and she would say a silent prayer I would somehow be healed. Going through paperwork one day she came across a document with my signature, and she could not hold back tears.

Our neighbors were a source of strength and support following my accident. Our next-door neighbors, Leo and Sheri, were very concerned. They periodically edged our lawn or cut our grass when necessary. Mike and Tess from across the street also helped with yard work, and Tess made me a rice-filled heating pad I regularly use as a neck warmer. Another Grapevine neighbor, David Clubb, was a physical therapy professional. He knew of a local foundation started by Joey Wilkins, a woman who had been paralyzed after a fall from a barn. Her foundation was established to help those in the Grapevine area living with spinal cord injuries. The Joey Wilkins Foundation hired a contractor who replaced the steps to our house with a concrete ramp, widened some doorways, and replaced our bathtub with a roll-in shower. We don't know what we would have done without help from those wonderful people, and we simply can't thank them enough.

The next three weeks became four because BIR could not get everything ready that quickly. They had me test a number of power wheelchairs, but I couldn't find a drive mechanism I was comfortable with. One activated movement when I lifted my head off the headrest, but the chair couldn't distinguish between leaning forward to look at something and a command to move. Another activated movement when my head pushed against the headrest, but I couldn't rest my head without triggering a motion command. Sip-and-Puff technology was apparently the tried-and-true mechanism over the years, but I could not get the hang of it. I was afraid someone or something was going to be in serious jeopardy with me at

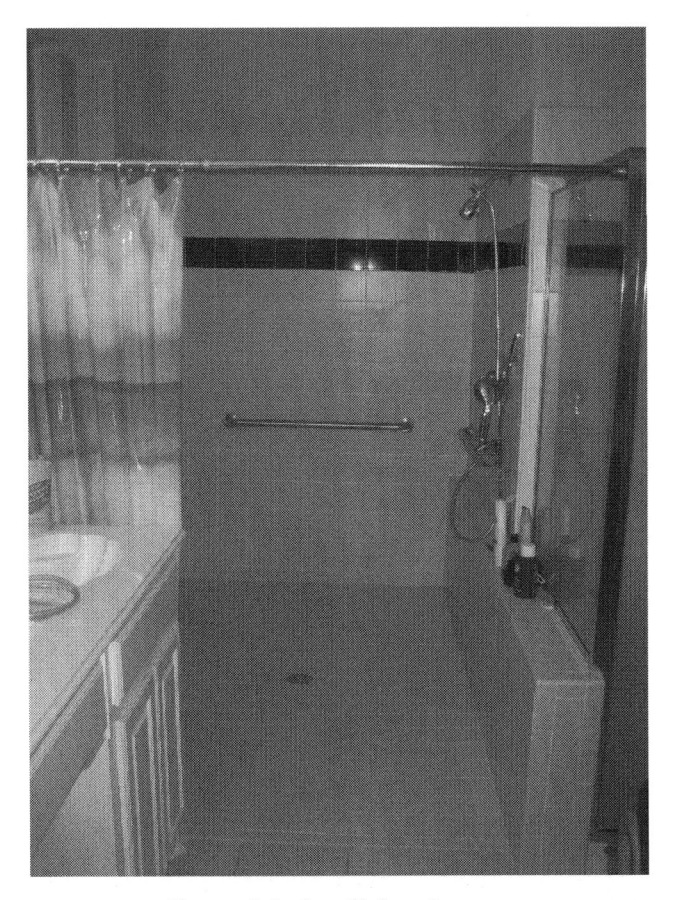

Remodeled roll in shower

the controls. Technicians described a mechanism operated with the tongue, but I had to commit to using it without testing it. This was because of hygiene considerations and the fact that it was custom-built for the individual. After all these trials, I was becoming discouraged. I was then shown a chin drive mechanism. Once I tested it, this proved to be the answer. It was an accelerator pedal, brake, and steering wheel, all operated by a joystick moved with your chin. A few days after our initial meeting with my caseworkers, it was the Fourth of July. At BIR it was just another day, but that evening they treated the spinal cord patients to a treat. They took us to the top floor where we had a commanding view of downtown Dallas and the fireworks show from Fair Park. I slumped to one side of my wheelchair and wasn't feeling very well, but I enjoyed the view. We were also entertained by Mike, one of the spinal cord patients. He maintained a steady banter. Much of it humorous, we couldn't help but laugh. He was a funny guy, and I enjoyed his humor the whole time I was at BIR. Everyone at rehab shared this one terrible thing, we all had in common but each person had their own unique story. Mike's story introduced me to a new world. I'm not sure if he was in a gang or not, but Mike had been shot five times and survived. Amazingly he was only a para—the term for those paralyzed from the waist down. This was his fifth attempt at rehab, and he seemed as if he really wanted to make it work. Apparently after each attempt he had returned to his old life, which involved a lot of drinking and drugs. He would tell stories about how bad autonomic dysreflexia was under the influence. This is something I still think of whenever I consume alcohol. Autonomic dysreflexia is a potentially life-threatening condition of the autonomic (involuntary) nervous system. It is characterized by the sudden onset of severe high blood pressure, a slow heart rate, and potential cognitive impairment. From what I understand, Mike pretty well kicked the drinking and drug habit after he left rehab. A couple years later, however, after I had started our foundation, I was contacted to see if anyone could use Mike's wheelchair and other specialized equipment. Unfortunately Mike had lost his battle with life. At the time I did not have a source to recycle equipment, but Mike's passing became the motivation to find a place where people could productively recycle their equipment so it could be safely used by others.

The remaining time at Baylor was a predictable cycle of physical and occupational therapy coupled with education classes about the care of spinal cord injuries. To improve my lung capacity, I had four daily sessions with a respiratory therapist. A nebulizer administered albuterol, which helped open my lungs. Immediately following that a respiratory therapist administered pressure coughs to clear my lungs.

Decreased lung capacity weakens the ability to cough and creates an increased chance of respiratory infections. A pressure cough involves someone applying firm and rapid pressure to the upper abdomen, forcing air out of the lungs. There was one particularly scary therapist. To administer pressure coughs, he would get on the bed and straddle me. Then he would push my chest with a wild look in his eye. He was a nice guy until it was game time. Then he turned into the Incredible Hulk!

One weekend Baylor took two vanloads of us to see a movie. The choices were *Mamma Mia* or *The Dark Knight*. A vote was taken, and *The Dark Knight* won in a landslide. It was a treat, but the real purpose was to help us acclimate to being in a wheelchair in public. I found the experience very uncomfortable. As soon as we got out of the vans, we were subjected to many stares. I could almost read their faces and tell what they were thinking. Others tried, almost too hard, to avoid looking at us. To this day I associate that film is with negative vibes. The event, however, accomplished its purpose. It forced me to mentally prepare for those interactions once I left the security of BIR. I have decided that, if people have difficulty talking with, engaging, or interacting with me because of my disability, it is their problem. I am more than happy to talk with anyone about my situation if he or she is curious, but I'll be damned if I'm going to feel diminished because of my condition.

One of the least productive sessions at BIR involved meetings with the rehab psychiatrist. She seemed concerned about my mental state and why I had not exhibited signs of depression and loss. I'm sure she was concerned that repressed feelings could explode later, but I didn't know what to tell her. I hated what had happened to me, but I was determined not to let it ruin my life or the lives of my family. In the years since my accident, I have read comments and books from some paralyzed people who say they wouldn't change a thing. If I were offered the opportunity not to be paralyzed, I would accept in a heartbeat! There are a lot of things I have seen, felt, and learned that I would want to keep, but the physical reality of being paralyzed is not one of them. In the years since my accident, there have been times when I succumbed to sadness and loss. These instances, however, are generally short-lived. They typically arise without warning, and virtually anything can trigger them. I might be watching a basketball game, and remember how it felt when I knew a shot was good the second it left my hand. Knowing I will never feel that again can hit me hard. I might be listening to someone describe an upcoming trip, knowing my ability to travel is severely compromised. As I get further removed from the accident, these feelings increasingly involve the impact on those around me. I think about the golf or racquetball games I won't be able to play with my sons, the college basketball games I have missed watching Christie play live, or the getaway weekends lost with Sue. I have found the best way to deal with these perfectly natural feelings is to indulge them briefly, and then remember I have a responsibility to be strong for those around me. I am still a father and husband, and I have to be thankful for every day I can continue to be a positive influence in those roles.

Christie's desktop

One thing that sustained me through those days, and still sustains me, is the tremendous support network I am truly blessed to have. I routinely received calls of support from people I had worked with over the years. Friends, neighbors, Christie's coaches, and parents of Christie's friends continued to bring over dinners, flowers, and restaurant gift cards. One of the volleyball parents even brought an edible arrangement to the hospital, and it came to symbolize the dichotomy of my situation. On the one hand, the gift represented the generosity and well wishes of many people. On the other hand, it represented the terrible fact of why it was even given. Rick Mang and Nathan Firmin, pastors at First United Methodist Church in Grapevine, were regular visitors, as were Marilyn Smith and her husband, Paul, from Christ United Methodist Church in Plano. Several people earned places in the "frequent visitor program," and they brightened my days immeasurably. My family was rock solid in their support, and I don't know where I would be without them. This event made our family stronger, but in too many cases, the opposite happens. Sue and Eric went through every element of rehab with me, learning how to do everything that would be necessary to keep me functioning and alive. Eric voluntarily left ACU and his football scholarship to move back home and help. I felt very bad he was unable to complete his days at ACU. I encouraged him not to make a rash decision, but he felt a strong sense of duty. He said there were times he used to feel he had missed out on something, but now he feels that not coming back would have meant missing so many more important things. He then enrolled in the University of North Texas and finished his degree in 2010. Christie was unfailingly there on evenings and weekends. She used her artistic capabilities to put together a desktop drawing on the ever-present laptop used for planning and communication. She always came up with a word of the day, which was a humorous addition to our whiteboard. Stephen came home every two weeks. He kept me company, told me about his experiences building a rail line in Yuma, and helped me find and make operational the voice-activated phone I still use. Sue was and continues to be my rock. She also has never looked back, never given up, and remained positive. She is the fulcrum of my support network, and I will never be able to thank her enough for coming into my life so many years ago.

I also enjoyed the support of some very good friends and siblings. Some friends even became like family. My sister Sue was and continues to be a huge ally and friend. It took a little while, but I came to realize these kinds of trauma don't just affect you. They affect everyone you know and each has his or her own way of coming to grips. Some do this without hesitation. Some do this awkwardly. Some never do, and some whom you thought cared really don't. People say an event like this develops character. rather I believe it reveals character. In the last five years, for better or worse, I have seen a lot of character revelation, and that includes my own.

It was finally time to come home, but we did not have a handicapped-accessible van. Baylor did not have a transportation service, which was a concern because they told us they could not provide a ride. We lived thirty or so miles from Baylor, but we figured, when push came to shove, they would find us transportation. Thankfully our home was ready courtesy of the Joey Wilkins Foundation and Grapevine AMBUCS. Joey was employed by the Grapevine Chamber of Commerce, and I saw her from time to time after my accident. Her enthusiasm for what she did was infectious. On the departure day, BIR staff helped load me in the van they originally weren't going to provide. On the ride home, I discovered what it must have been like to ride in Conestoga wagons! It was my first long ride in a wheelchair vehicle, and it was a bit scary. We took one bump sufficiently hard to bounce my arm off the wheelchair, and it was hanging down by my side. While disconcerting it didn't particularly hurt. I would discover that was not always the case. I notified the driver, who pulled over and crawled back to remedy the problem. At long last we pulled up in front of the home I had left six weeks before for a quick bike ride.

9

HOME AT LAST

It was a warm, August day when I returned home. The first thing I did was look at the ramps, widened doorways, and remodeled bath funded by the Joey Wilkins Foundation and Grapevine AMBUCS. Without that I would not have been able to get back into my own home. Baylor had arranged to supply me with loaner equipment until permanent items could be supplied, including a power wheelchair, Hoyer Lift, bed, and shower chair. Because of the tight clearances and a ninety-degree turn, I could not drive myself into the bedroom without tearing up walls, so Eric drove me in. The first thing I noticed were two twin beds in our room where there had been one queen bed. That was when it dawned on me that Sue and I would no longer be able to sleep on the same bed. After twenty-six years of sharing the same bed, it was a sad realization.

Now that I was back home, Sue could resume working. At times, however, the immensity of the past six weeks would suddenly penetrate her reality like an unwelcome guest. While working at her desk and totally immersed in work, she would sometimes imagine me walking into the office. She wished she could trade places and give me able-bodied time and relief, even if only for a few minutes.

Gently rubbing the top of my shoulders became a new gesture of endearment.

Before my injury Sue had been working from home three days and commuting to Plano the other two. Her employer, Mike Ridley, now graciously consented to let her work from home five days a week. Clients calling in would never know she was not at the office, yet she would be nearby if something happened to me. I didn't need intense monitoring, but I was incapable of doing anything for myself. Due to the paralysis, my lungs have lost a significant portion of their pre-injury capacity. Fluid regularly collects in my lungs, and I can't cough sufficiently to clear them. With Sue being nearby, she can give me a pressure cough. Sue has been with her employer, an insurance agent, for ten years and is a valuable member of their staff, so this was very much a win-win arrangement. That first week home, I relished going back to home cooking. I had lost thirty pounds since the accident, which was a good thing, but it was primarily because I didn't like hospital food. Late in my stay at BIR, I found out I had been mistakenly put on a restricted diet. I discovered this because I rebelled one day against a terrible sandwich that looked like an unidentifiable piece of meat on white bread. That led to a conversation with the nutritionist and the resultant discovery. Being on a restricted diet was good for losing weight but terrible from a taste standpoint. I was rather disappointed however that the home cooking I was so looking forward to just didn't taste as good as I thought it would. That was a harbinger of things to come.

Baylor stressed the importance of continuing physical and occupational therapy, and insurance covered it for the first ninety days. Twice a week Baylor sent Kathy out for physical therapy and Tommy for occupational therapy. On Kathy's third visit, we were chatting away during exercise when I noticed her frown. "What's wrong," I asked.

"You have blood clots," she said matter-of-factly.

When I was at Parkland, one of my follow-up operations was to put a filter in the vena cava artery to block blood clots from flowing into my lungs or heart. "Doesn't the filter protect me," I asked.

"Not necessarily," she answered, still frowning. "I'm concerned about DVT." Deep vein thrombosis is a condition in which a blood clot forms in one or more of the body's deep veins. It is usually in the legs. She performed a few more checks and said she wanted to call a doctor at Baylor. The doctor confirmed her diagnosis, and she told me we needed to go to the hospital. My heart sank, and I tried to reason with her. Sue came in, and the three of us discussed it. Finally we decided to go, albeit reluctantly. We did not have a handicapped-accessible van and had only practiced transferring me from a wheelchair to a car once at Baylor. During that one attempt, it took four people to get me into the Crown Vic Baylor used as a model. Neither Kathy nor Sue felt comfortable trying to get me into our Honda Accord. We decided to call an ambulance, and in short order it was in front of the house. One of the EMTs said he had helped transport me to Parkland following my accident. As I lay on my back and was wheeled out, I looked at one of the diffusers high on the ceiling. I wondered how long it would be before I saw it again.

Once we arrived at the hospital, I was taken to an ER room, and the interminable wait began. School had ended for the day, and Christie joined us about the time a nurse came in to perform an ultrasound on my legs. I looked at the screen, but I could not pick anything out. During the ultrasound we talked with the nurse about blood clots, finally asking her if she was finding any. "I'm not supposed to say anything," she said. "The doctor is supposed to give the prognosis." After relentless prodding from the three of us, she finally told us I did have blood clots, and they would admit me. With that we discussed the need for an alternating pressure mattress to avoid getting a pressure sore. A pressure sore is an area of skin that breaks down from staying in one position too long.

This is a constant concern with paralyzed individuals. She said she would add that to the charts and make sure we got one. Eric called after work, and we told him the news. As it was about dinnertime, he stopped at Panda Express and picked up dinner for everyone, which we ate in the ER. Shortly after I was admitted and moved to a room upstairs.

It felt like BIR all over again with one exception. I could control the TV channel at BIR using assistive technology, but I could not at Baylor Grapevine. That meant watching programs I wasn't interested in unless I was lucky enough to catch an attendant willing to change the channel. Sue, Christie, and Eric were regular visitors, stopping in multiple times each day. Sue regularly stayed overnight, which provided both of us with consolation. Eric and one of the hospital employees would put me in a wheelchair, and we would go down to the hospital cafeteria. It was the highlight of the day. One evening, as Sue was moving through the room, she tripped over something and fell hard. The fall broke her finger, and we urged her to have it X-rayed. She didn't want to at first but finally agreed. It was a bad break that required orthopedic surgery, which she had a few days later. She had never broken any bones prior to this.

About three days into my stay, the activity in my room and visits by previously unseen medical personnel indicated potential trouble. Finally a doctor I didn't know introduced himself and told me I had MRSA, a methicillin-resistant staph infection that's resistant to the antibiotics commonly used to treat ordinary staph infections. As a result visitors had to don protective equipment that looked like chemical warfare suits. The notice put on my room's door looked like a scarlet letter. I felt a kinship with people in a leper colony. All this extended my stay another week. When I came home and looked up at the same diffuser, I felt confident I was home for good.

Christmas 2008

During the day Sue worked, and I watched TV. I had never been a huge TV watcher, but now I didn't have much choice. That was when I discovered cable news. I had periodically watched CNN when I was traveling but was unaware of all the other cable news channels. I watched Fox, MSNBC, and CNN. I quickly discovered there wasn't twenty-four hours of news to cover, but it was being covered anyway and with bias to boot. I also watched the History Channel, Discovery Channel, and others with worthwhile programming. I was aware of voice-activated computer software, but I knew it was going to be some time before I had access to it. In the meantime TV was my constant companion. I was determined to use it strictly for productive purposes, either keeping up with the news or watching educational programs.

In September our good friends Mike and Karen Secor organized a personal benefit with Dennis and Karen McGuffie and

Mark and Teri Tatum to help with our medical expenses. It was held on the top floor of a building with great views of downtown Dallas. Hors d'oeuvres were served, and there was a large turnout for the silent auction fundraiser. Mark Tatum donated some sports memorabilia such as a soccer ball signed by Pele through his employer, Genesco Sports Enterprises. I had never been the recipient of charity, so it was a humbling experience, but we were very grateful for it. In the spring of 2009, a personal golf tournament benefit was held at Tanglewood Golf Course on Lake Texoma. This was sponsored by Vicki and John LaPlant, Mike Hajduk, Mark Tatum, and Bonnie Maupin. Mike and Bonnie were friends I had known for many years, dating to our employment at Lennox. Proceeds from these events enabled us to purchase a handicapped-accessible van, shower chair, and other durable medical equipment not covered by insurance. Anything labeled "durable medical equipment" or "assistive technology" is ridiculously expensive, so I simply cannot describe the degree of gratitude we felt following these events. We are truly thankful for all our friends who made these magnificent events possible.

Two of my nagging and recurring problems were fever and chills. Without warning I would start getting cold, and that would lead to chills. Sue would pile three or four blankets on top of me while I shivered and my teeth chattered. After about three hours, the trend would go the other way, and I would start to get hot. My body temperature would fluctuate from about 96 to 101. While at BIR I had experienced some of that, but they told me it was normal with a spinal cord injury. By Thanksgiving, however, things seemed to be out of control. The cycles were more frequent, and the temperature swings were getting wider. On Thanksgiving Day I was in the living room watching a football game when the chills started. Within an hour my teeth were chattering, and I felt miserable. Sue piled on the blankets, and we started up the fire which I sat in front of. Predictably my temperature began to swing the other way, peaking

HOME AT LAST

at 102 degrees. This continued into the next day and evening, and my temperature elevated to104 degrees around ten p.m. Sue insisted we go to the hospital, so she and Eric got me out of bed, and we left for the place I have come to dread.

We had the usual long wait in the emergency room. I slumped in my wheelchair and tried to sleep. When I was finally called into an exam room, the nurse took my temperature and other vitals. Periodically leaving the room, she finally came back and told me we needed to keep an eye on it, but otherwise we could go back home. I felt as if we had wasted our time. I hated going to a doctor only to be told there was nothing wrong. Back at home I went to bed, and I continued the fever and chills cycle. By Sunday night it was still raging out of control, and one temperature reading spiked at 105 degrees. Once again we went to the emergency room. The wait didn't seem as long, though. Possibly this was because I looked so bad. When the nurse took my temperature and blood pressure, activity quickened. Shortly thereafter I was told I would be admitted to the ICU. Once again we were back in the hospital, but I felt so bad I didn't really care. The next day I was assigned an infectious disease doctor. As it turned out, I once again had MRSA, which necessitated the visitor space suits. Things took a more ominous turn when I was told I also had sepsis—a potentially life-threatening complication of an infection. The inflammation could trigger a cascade of changes and damage multiple organ systems, even causing them to fail. At odd hours and without notice, I would be taken off for an MRI, a nuclear medicine scan, or a variety of other tests designed to pinpoint the source of the sepsis. I don't know if specialists purposely avoid the day shift, but all these night tests did not lead to restful sleep. Despite their best efforts, the source of my sepsis was never found, frustrating the doctor and lengthening my stay. I was put on an IV antibiotic considered a last-ditch defense against sepsis. If it failed there was nothing the doctors could do. It was a helpless feeling to look at the IV connected to my body and know it was the only thing standing between my life and death. All I could do was pray it would be effective. I was on a high-risk floor, and I heard Code Blue called with some degree of regularity. Following one such call, I heard commotion and then a lady crying from a room just down the hall. About an hour later, I saw a grim-faced man dressed in black with a purple blanket walking down the hall. Shortly after a stretcher with a body wrapped in a purple body bag rolled past my doorway, and that's when I realized what all the commotion had been about. Two more times during my stay this scenario was repeated on my floor. Each time I thought of the families, internalizing what they must have been going through. It brought home a lot of stark realities. It reminded me to slow down enough to truly appreciate those ordinary moments in life. I couldn't help but wonder if my life ended on that floor, what would it have stood for? I offered a silent prayer for the family and the lost loved one.

Christmas was fast approaching, and I was determined not to spend it in the hospital. The doctor, however, was reluctant to release me until I displayed no more symptoms and he knew the source of the infection. Eventually we achieved the former without the latter, and I was released about two weeks after being admitted. Discharge day seemed to validate the power of prayer for Sue and me. This type of infection is fatal for too many people with spinal cord injuries, particularly in the first twelve months after injury. I was anxious to do something Christmasy after two weeks in the hospital, so the following weekend, with Stephen home, we all went to a nearby mall. We weren't shopping for anything. We just enjoyed the Christmas music and being in the moment. I didn't even mind the crowds and traffic. As we strolled through the mall, we came across a hot pretzel vendor. For some reason that sounded like an insanely good idea, so we purchased some. One thing that stands out about Christmas 2008 is how good that pretzel tasted. Over the next couple of weeks, it dawned on me my taste buds were back. Everything tasted like it used to. As much as anything, that was how I knew I had finally defeated that infection. In retrospect I believe it had been plaguing me since I was at BIR in July. In all I had lost sixty pounds since my accident, and I was in the mood to put my newly found taste buds to good use. Christmas passed, and within a blink of an eye, it was New Year's Eve. 2008 could not be gone fast enough.

10

A NEW LIFE

Prior to World War II, most people who had incurred spinal cord injuries didn't survive the trauma. If they did, they typically developed debilitating pressure sores or kidney or bladder problems, which resulted in infections and death. Doctor Howard Rusk was the driving force behind changing this. During World War II, Rusk served in the air corps, and that exposed him to seriously wounded and disabled servicemen. These individuals were typically discharged after treatment and dumped into the Veterans Administration, where they received custodial care until they inevitably died. Rusk believed these men did not have to become charity cases. Newly developed antibiotics could keep previously fatal infections at bay, but more importantly he believed a comprehensive rehabilitation program, encompassing emotional, social, educational, and occupational needs, could produce useful and productive citizens. He won the military over, but Rusk was frustrated by postwar resistance he encountered from the medical establishment. He found a receptive audience, however, at New York University, and with additional private funding, he set out to create the rehabilitation program he envisioned. He created the Institute of

Physical Medicine and Rehabilitation, the first facility of its kind in the United States. He had one rule at the institute. No one could tell a patient what he or she couldn't do.

One of his early patients was Roy Campanella. Roy was a Hall of Fame baseball player for the Brooklyn Dodgers. Along with Jackie Robinson, he was a pioneer in breaking the color barrier in major league baseball. Considered one of the greatest catchers in the game's history, Roy was paralyzed in a motor vehicle accident in January of 1958. Paralyzed at the C5-C6 vertebrae, Roy was considered lucky. One inch higher at the C3-C4 vertebrae and he would have died. My injury was at the C3-C4 vertebrae, and I consider myself lucky. One inch higher, and I either would not have survived or would have been vent-dependent like Christopher Reeve.

I did survive, however, and for the first time in six months, we were free from the clutches of an immediate medical crisis. It was January of 2009, the holidays were over, and all the friends and family had gone back to their lives. This was the dreaded time I knew would come. I literally looked at myself in the mirror across the room and soberly assessed the facts.

- I was fifty-three years old.
- I was paralyzed and completely dependent upon others for everything. Forever.
- I had no job and no viable prospects for getting another one.
- My life consisted of lying in bed all day and watching TV.

The ultimate question was what I was going to do with the rest of my life.

Imagine for a minute looking in a mirror and telling yourself these things. If some degree of chill doesn't come over you, there's something wrong with you! For the first time since my accident, I could face these unpleasant facts head-on without the constant distraction of health issues. Thinking about this in the abstract scared me. What if I lived twenty-five more years and never found anything worthwhile to do? How could I keep from being bored out of my mind and driving both Sue and myself crazy? These thoughts crept into my mind. I decided however I could not focus on the problem in the aggregate. Drawing on techniques I had used at work when taking on large, complicated problems, I began to engage in creative thought. I started to think about the assets I could bring to bear on this situation. Being fifty-three meant I had the energy to build something with the help of numerous friends and contacts. While physically incapable of anything, I still had my mind. After spending a week with those poor souls on the traumatic brain injury floor, I was ever so grateful for that. During autumn Pat and I agreed returning to my position at PCI was not feasible. That was an important decision for both of us. I needed to face that reality, and Pat needed the freedom to fill my position for the company. Even though my medical condition was now stable, job prospects looked about as bleak as a Chicago blizzard. I had the security of a long-term disability policy taken out while I was at PCI Industries, and that provided us with great peace of mind. While not anywhere near the income I made when I worked, the combination of Sue's salary and the long-term disability policy allowed us to stay in our home. I began the process of working with the state of Texas to receive assistive technology, and while it would be a while before that came through, I knew my days of lying in bed and watching TV were numbered.

That important question still had to be answered. What was I going to do? Problems seem at their worst when they are the sole focus of one's thoughts. Things immediately improve however when you mentally shift to a solutions mind-set. From my life experiences, including the most recent ones learned from hospital stays, I knew my focus had to be outward and pointed toward others. Beyond a certain curiosity, people were not going to be interested in my health issues, and I did not want these to be my focus either. But what then could I focus outward on? I had spent thirty-five years building a career in the HVAC industry. I had friends and contacts all over the United States. I felt as if what I had done mattered and made a difference. I had no inclination to strike out in an unrelated field. Rather I wanted to maintain these contacts in a way that was meaningful to both them and me. In many ways I felt like I was retired at an early age. I reexamined former thoughts about what I had wanted to do in retirement. I had never thought about it that seriously, but in general terms I knew I wanted to do something philanthropic. I wanted to stay involved in the HVAC industry, and I wanted to write. I definitely felt I had been blessed in so many ways, and if I were to leave this earth without helping others, my life journey would be incomplete. I thought about individuals in situations like mine. According to the Christopher & Dana Reeve Foundation, six million Americans are living with some form of paralysis, and approximately twelve thousand individuals join their ranks every year. That's one in fifty people. That's the same number as the combined populations of Los Angeles, Philadelphia, and Washington, DC. In a visceral sense, I knew these people. I understood what they were going through. That was when the idea coalesced. I could use my background and contacts to help others in my situation who were less fortunate. I even had a working model I could study. The Joey Wilkins Foundation, which had been so important to us at a critical time, now provided both the inspiration and a working example for what I could do.

Until I acquired the tools to help make this vision a reality, I had to deal with the present. Christie was now a junior, and her basketball games on Tuesdays and Fridays offered welcome relief from the tedium of watching TV. I would get up on those days, and Sue and I would attend her games after work, usually grabbing a bite somewhere along the way. Getting out of the chair after one of those January events, we accidentally tore the valve on my wheelchair's Roho cushion. A Roho cushion is the seat on the wheelchair, and it is made up of dozens of air pockets. These seats have been proven to prevent pressure sores for people sitting in wheelchairs. Tearing the valve turned out to be a very costly mistake. The loaner wheelchair had a leather backup seat. Not knowing any different, we put the leather seat on the chair. A week or so later, I developed a serious pressure sore on my backside. The people who supplied us with the chair later told us the leather seat was not meant to be used. Only a Roho cushion could be used. This, however, was not covered by insurance and cost five hundred dollars to replace. The pressure sore turned out to be the bigger problem. The wound had nearly gone to the bone, and the doctor prescribed a wound VAC, which I had to wear everywhere for two months. As bad as that was, it prevented a very unpleasant surgery. A big concern was infection. If the wound became infected, and the infection reached the bone, the situation would be life-threatening. The wound VAC did its job, but it was a year before the wound was completely healed. We are now hypersensitive to this issue. All it takes is one day in the wheelchair where something is putting pressure on my body, and I will develop a pressure sore that takes months to heal. Since that time I have developed four or five more, but we have always caught them in the early stages. Since I cannot feel anything below my shoulders, I don't know when I am being exposed to undue pressure. Seeing a wound care doctor within twenty-four to forty-eight hours of the first signs is key to mitigating the damage. There is no foolproof way to avoid the problem other than hyper vigilance. The worst part about getting a pressure sore is having to spend more time in bed. In my case pressure sores have always come from being in the wheelchair. I typically only spend about twenty hours a week in my chair, so any loss of this time is a real letdown. I highly value the two days a week I get up in my chair. On the other hand, I cannot imagine the toll on my body if I spent eight to ten hours a day and five to seven days a week in my chair. That schedule would literally kill me.

The 2009 Winter Olympics provided some relief from boredom, but after they were over, it was back to news channels, sports, and old movies. I began to check out books on tape from the local library, and friends sent me some as well. The hardest part of listening to a book on tape in bed is not falling asleep. I must admit that happened more often than not. Becoming a quadriplegic has the feeling of being in a broken-down car on the roadside. Everyone is driving by, and their lives are busy and full. Every now and then, one of them pulls over to spend some time only to get back in their car and zoom off. Some well-intentioned friends sent me books to read, but I needed someone to read them to me. Where I could catch an hour or so with Sue or the kids, we put it to use on the computer. I would dictate and reply to e-mails, and I began correspondence with my sister Sue about the requirements for setting up a 501(c)(3). Meaningful progress on setting up a foundation had to wait, however, until I could procure voice-activated equipment. Within a fairly short period of time, the family settled into a workable pattern. Between Eric and Christie, we had all the in-home care we needed and utilized no outside assistance. That was a wonderful luxury but one we knew would not last forever.

While my sister continued to research forming a foundation, I began to talk with various friends and industry veterans about becoming members of the board. Vicki and John LaPlant had been proponents from the outset, and Mike Hajduk and Mark Tatum were right behind. I had worked with Mike in the early '90s at Lennox, and Mark was a family friend. I knew they were indispensable to what we were trying to build from scratch. As an interesting side note, Sue's firm provided insurance to Ann McClamrock, who answered phones for Mike. Ann's son was a quadriplegic from a high school football injury. Sue had spoken with Ann many times about her son and looked up to both of them as role models. May and June were spent developing policy documents and replying to IRS questions about our original submission. The work would have been impossible had I not had my wife Sue, Eric, or Christie to work the computer for me. Working in this way made me extremely anxious to acquire voice-activated software. We received our 501(c)(3) designation the second week in July. We were in business! I also received the voice-activated software, which allowed me to interface with my computer. Coupled with my voice-activated cell phone, I began to get excited about the future. My days of lying unproductively in bed were over. I could really begin to live my new life.

As the first anniversary of my accident approached, I had a feeling of dread. It wasn't an anniversary to be celebrated, but I knew June 15 had forever joined the list of unforgettable dates in my life. During that first year, I had many people tell me the accident had been God's will and that things happen for a reason. While I never offered a contrarian view to these comments, I don't believe either of them. I don't believe anyone is predestined for anything. Rather we have free will to choose our direction in life. I don't believe in a God who looks down on his creation and says, "Sam, on June 15 you're going to buy a lottery ticket that will make you a millionaire. Joe, you're going to take a bike ride that will cause you to be paralyzed." People have asked me if I am angry with God. I am not because I don't think God did this to me. I have heard people wonder why God allows terrible things such as Hitler or paralysis to happen. It is my belief God does not choose to do these things. I believe he created us with free will, and we are consequently each responsible for our own actions. I wasn't programmed from the moment of my birth to one day be paralyzed. I chose to take a bike ride one day and simply had an accident. I could have chosen to take a swim or sit out by the pool and have a beer instead. To believe we are somehow predestined to an outcome diminishes us. We are, after all, the crown jewels of God's creation. I have never prayed for a cure because I don't think it's what is most important now. I have prayed for those closest to me whom this accident has profoundly impacted and for my ongoing health and utility. That's what's most important now. I have also prayed to be spared from the ravages of someday being old, alone, broke, in pain, and paralyzed—, a fate many people unfortunately do find themselves living. No matter how bad off we are, the odds are extremely high someone is worse off than ourselves. We each have a lot to be thankful for, regardless of our condition.

These were not the thoughts going through my mind on the one-year anniversary. When the date came, I didn't mention it to anyone until later in the day. When the time rolled around to 5:17 p.m., I allowed myself some time to be sad. I shed some tears thinking about what was lost. I am still haunted by how much this has changed Sue's life. Her plans and dreams have changed because of a stupid bicycle accident. It hardly seems right. We still have each other, however, and we have to value every moment together. Grief is a healthy and necessary place to occasionally visit, but one cannot live there. After about a half hour, I forced myself to move on, reminding myself of the pledge I made on the trail one year earlier.

I don't know if the next generation of technology will provide effective work-arounds for paralysis or even cure it, but I think Howard Rusk would be pleased to see how far things have progressed.

11

HITTING OUR STRIDE

People with spinal cord injuries, especially those with high-level lesions, typically have a lot of spasticity. Sometimes that can be mistaken for movement, but it is involuntary, and it can hurt. It is mitigated by a medicine called baclofen, which I was taking orally. By the fall of 2009, doctors decided the amount I was taking was insufficient to combat my increasing spasticity and that additional oral dosages were inappropriate. The solution was something known as an intrathecal baclofen pump. This delivers baclofen directly to the base of my spinal cord in continuous, programmable amounts. The dosage is also significantly less than that taken orally because it does not have to be processed by the kidneys. The disadvantage is that it has to be surgically implanted. We agreed to the procedure, and with some trepidation I checked into Baylor Irving to have it done. They first injected the dosage into my spinal cord as a test. The test was successful, and I was scheduled for surgery the next day. The next morning I was prepped and taken to surgery, which was something I was getting too used to. Everything went as planned, and I was taken to the ICU afterward. Apparently that is standard procedure following surgery on someone in my condition.

Everything went well that afternoon, and after dinner Christie came for a visit. We went through her math homework, though, I'm not sure I was much help. I had to spend one more night due to fever and nausea, after which my symptoms cleared. When I checked out, I was virtually free of the spasms that had become so troublesome.

I had to see a specialist every month to have the medicine checked and refilled, which was a nuisance given the coordination, time, and effort required to simply get me up. There are not many doctors trained to handle Medtronic intrathecal pumps, and our doctor was a novice. When we would go in for our monthly appointment, a Medtronic representative was always at her side. This was probably a good thing. The doctor always had difficulty finding my internal pump, which she would do by probing with a needle. Thankfully I can't feel anything, so the only real casualty was excess bleeding. Following our move a little more than a year later, I had to find a new slate of doctors. The new baclofen pump specialist changed the formula, which allowed me to go six months between appointments. This was a major advantage. After all, every time I have to see a doctor, we have to schedule home health to help me get up, and Sue has to take time off work. In five years I will have to have the pump replaced, something I am not looking forward to. In the meantime, however, this amazing device provides significant relief from a condition that will be my lifetime companion.

The fall of 2009 and spring of 2010 were pretty uneventful, except for a handful of medical events. During the spring I contracted pneumonia, which is scary for someone in my condition because of my already reduced lung capacity.

In the fall of 2010, Eric graduated from college and accepted a full-time position from a logistics firm for whom he had been interning. He got an apartment and moved away from home. In addition Christie left for college on a basketball scholarship. While we were delighted for them, it meant adjustments for us. For nearly two and a half years, we had been completely self-sufficient. Eric, Christie, and Sue had mastered all the skills necessary to take care of my various needs. Their knowledge was easily superior to a certified nurse's assistant. With them leaving we needed to begin a relationship with a home health company. Getting me up and into my wheelchair or getting me back in bed is a two-person job so we needed to find a reliable firm.

In-home care today is provided by companies with soothing names such as Visiting Angels, Heaven at Home, In-Home Companions, and others. Ads for these companies depict mature, caring employees virtually doting on the every need of their charges. Caregiver and patient are shown laughing and engaging in easy conversation. They promise stable, long-lasting caregivers with warm personalities.

Once again I approached the problem as I would have in business. I conducted extensive research on local companies, interviewed the top candidates by phone, and prioritized the finalists. The individuals the first company introduced to us were downright scary. The owner brought out a lady for us to meet. He said she would be a good fit for our situation, but she had difficulty looking anyone in the eye, and during the interview she stared off into space. She did not offer confidence-inspiring answers to any question, and this was his best foot forward. Sue and I looked at each other, sharing the same unspoken thought. We told the owner we would give this lady an opportunity, if for no other reason than to give her the benefit of the doubt. She came out twice and never showed up again. Our relationship with that company was short-lived, and we moved to another on our list, with which we have had a much better experience. Our capabilities are seen as negative when working with home health agencies. They want a patient who requires the caregiver to spend a lot of time. Our needs are much more minimal. We only need someone for showers and transfers. On the flip side, Sue and I are competent and easy to get along with, and that makes us desirable customers.

We learned early on not to get too attached to any caregiver. In the past forty months, we have worked with twenty-five different caregivers. The trend over the last twenty-four months, however, has been much better. This applies to the length of time we have worked with a caregiver and the quality of that caregiver. The lives of caregivers are difficult. The pay is low, and if they don't work in a facility, they are constantly driving to different patient's homes. It is typically not a career position, yet the demand for them is high and growing. The situation is difficult for the patients as well. When one gets to the point of needing a caregiver, one is either physically and/or mentally compromised. That means the person is in a situation where he or she cannot afford to pay out large sums of money, and typically insurance covers none of these services. The coming wave of baby boomers who will increasingly need these services portends a looming crisis. Additionally many people have not accumulated sufficient retirement portfolios to meet their coming needs. The nature of the business squeezes the margins of the companies hiring these caregivers, and turnover is an ongoing problem for them and their patients. For us this means constantly retraining new employees on some of the most basic aspects of care. Home health companies could greatly benefit by strategically staffing their back offices and providing a modicum of training to their field employees. Currently everything appears to be on-the-job training. For patients like us that would provide greater peace of mind. For companies, this would greatly reduce the time spent managing easily avoided crises, providing the owner with more time for business development.

By fall 2010 we were empty nesters in a four-bedroom home with a pool that was wasted on two people, neither of whom were swimmers. Living in such a dwelling, we quickly learned there is an inverse relationship between the amount of people living at home and the work required for upkeep. We had anticipated this scenario and began to research alternative options in early summer 2010. Broadly speaking our options were to move into an existing home or build a new one. Despite having lived in eight homes over the course of our marriage, we did not build any of them. We had three simple criteria for any new location—excellent accessibility, good energy efficiency, and low exterior maintenance. We ruled out existing homes pretty quickly based on this and turned our attention to building a new home. I researched builders relative to location, affordability, quality, and willingness to make changes to their floor plans. Two builders and locations came to the forefront in fairly short order. After talking with the both builders, the decision was no contest. One of these companies was building energy-efficient patio homes in a community just north of Plano, where we had lived for many years. The builder was very accommodating of the fairly significant changes we wanted to make, and they truly took an interest in our needs. While the move would provide significant relief for Sue, we still faced fall and winter in a home that needed its gutters cleaned, its leaves raked, and its pool maintained. It was the first fall Sue had ever faced this task alone, and the experience provided all the confirmation we needed that moving was the right choice. We were fortunate that fall to have a male home health care aide. He did not mind doing some yard work, but the bulk of it still fell on Sue. It killed me not to be able to handle any of this. My injury was life-changing for me and Sue, and situations such as this highlighted that fact. I don't often mourn my situation, but when I do it is as much for Sue as it is for me.

In February 2011 we moved into our new David Weekley home. We couldn't have been happier with the process or the outcome. In addition to gaining some welcome relief by moving, Sue's sister Nancy comes over almost every Saturday to help. That allows Sue to go out for an extended period to run errands and the like. It is about the only break she ever gets from monitoring my care, and it is a part of the week she always looks forward to. While I don't need continuous monitoring, I do always need someone available to give me a pressure cough or other potential assistance.

Moving to a new area meant finding new doctors. Before my injury I had always been healthy, and I only occasionally saw our primary care physician. In addition to finding a new primary care physician, I needed to find a baclofen specialist, podiatrist, gastroenterologist, urologist, dermatologist, and wound care specialist. Only my neurologist didn't change. It is as if many of the heretofore functioning systems in my body have gone on a sympathy strike with the spinal cord. I was surprised how many local physicians did not take Medicare, and I wondered how this foreshadowed things to come. Medically I had fallen into a pattern of not seeing any doctor for three or four months and then needing to see multiple specialists during the ensuing six weeks or so.

One condition that plagues people with paralysis is urinary tract infections. Despite our best efforts and following the doctor's instructions, I get them every two to three months. The symptoms include the cycle of fever and chills I struggled with in 2008, so we jump on them right away. In order to get an antibiotic to treat the infection, I have to get into the urologist to provide a test sample. Typically they want me to make an appointment, which might not be for several days. One or more days in my situation can mean a rapid deterioration, and because of home health scheduling requirements and Sue's job, we can't drop everything and make an appointment when someone cancels. Our solution is to take a sample as soon as the symptoms appear and drop it off at the urologist's office. It can then be screened sufficiently to allow a prescription to be written. The urologist's staff throw up roadblocks every time, but we eventually get them to see the medical necessity from our perspective. Every time we have taken a sample to be tested, it has been positive, so we know what we are doing. My parents' generation was raised to respect if not revere doctors. They never questioned their advice. Today that is no longer the case, particularly for anyone with a specialty medical condition. Patients have a responsibility to learn as much as they can about their personal conditions and advocate accordingly. Failure to do so puts yourself at an unacceptable risk. I shudder when I think of all the elderly people with one or more major conditions who can't or won't do this. It is not just the doctor who has to get the patient. Equally important is the office staff. At present we are on our third urologist, and so far this one seems to truly understand our plight. The tenacity developed growing up in a family of eleven and living in close quarters at a high school seminary prepared me well for these situations. I can understand why many get overwhelmed by the medical system, from providers to medical billing. Fortunately I am able to stay on top of all this. Thanks to Dragon technology and my Sip-and-Puff phone, I can largely shield Sue from the burden of dealing with appointments, billing and insurance.

As I have become comfortable in my new skin, I find reactions to me fascinating. Most interesting are innocent little children with no inhibitions. When they look at me in public, they are fascinated. Meanwhile their parents are typically the inverse. Terrified by what they might have to explain to their children, they can't seem to get them away from me fast enough. On a few occasions, I've had children walk up to me and start a conversation. They typically ask something like, "Are you hurt?" I enjoy talking with them and helping them understand. When it is too late for their parents to make a clean getaway, the angst on their face is clearly visible. When they see I am not stressed by the situation however, they become more relaxed. A similar situation occurs for people who come to the house when I am in bed. I suspect some don't come because of their unease, although I enjoy all visits. The two most memorable interactions I've had as a wheelchair occupant involve an older lady and a young boy. One Sunday in Grapevine after church, Sue and I were in the lobby and talking with some people. A lady came up to Sue, took her hand, and sorrowfully asked, "How is he doing?" She never even looked at me. The other situation occurred in our neighborhood. We were talking with a young mother who had just arrived home from school with her children. Sue was talking with the mom, and her young son was standing at her side. At one point I offered a comment, and the boy's eyes got very wide. He exclaimed, "He talks!" It turned out there was a wheelchair-bound child in his class who could not talk, so the boy thought anyone in a wheelchair was unable to speak. Recently we were in a restaurant, and after taking everyone else's order, the waitress without ever looking at me asked Sue, "What would he like?" From now on my response will be to repeat what the little boy told me!

Forty or fifty years ago, those who predicted flying cars by now would be disappointed. What they would have missed, however, is the incredible effect technology has come to play in nearly every aspect of our lives. To prevent pressure sores in Roy Campanella's day, patients were confined to a Stryker bed. These beds allowed the patient to be turned every few hours, "like a piece of ham between two pieces of bread," according to Campanella. In my case I have a rotating air mattress that allows me to spend a long time in bed without being turned or rolled. That provides Sue and me with a significant measure of relief. Without that type of mattress, which Medicare doesn't pay for, the caregiver would have to turn the patient *every* two hours 24/7.

Normally I get up on Wednesdays or whatever day I have a doctor appointment. I also get up on Sunday, and we go to church and get together with friends and family. These two days also allow me some time to run free with no one around. There is a large nature preserve attached to our subdivision, and when I go back in there, I forget I'm in the midst of a large, urban environment. Going there takes me to a place of serenity; much like Winton Woods did in high school. It is also pretty secluded, so if I had a personal or equipment issue, that could be a problem. I am connected with a cell phone, so if something were to come up I can always call for assistance. Even twenty years ago this would have been unimaginable. The prospect of spending 75 percent of my waking hours in bed could be daunting and depressing, but technology changes the whole equation. In addition to the Dragon and cell phone technologies, environmental controls allow me to command my surrounding space. I can turn on and off lights, fans, and the TV, and I can change the position of my bed for comfort. For someone with a lower-level injury, he or she can also use these controls to open or close exterior doors and effectively live alone.

One thing I had not been able to do as much as I wanted is read. As a child I was a voracious reader, and after my injury I had the time but not the ability. A number of well-intentioned people sent me books, but I had to find someone with the time to sit with me and turn the pages. The Kindle application for computers has completely changed that. I now read a book every two months or so and always have one I am working on. I have even checked out Kindle books from local libraries. I have also converted all my publications to e-versions, allowing me to keep up with business and trade news. I regularly attend webinars on a wide range of subjects. This is yet another way to keep up with what is going on in the world. Whether reading or working, music enhances life like nothing else, and with Internet radio I can listen to any genre imaginable while I work. Life-enhancing technology can also be of a simpler variety. Quadriplegics need to drink a lot of fluids, so Stephen connected a Camelback hydration pack to the bed, which provides a constant source of freshwater. An additional advantage is that the mechanism connecting the Camelback tubing is available to scratch itches on my nose and face. Itches represent one of life's major inconveniences for quadriplegics, so maybe it's a good thing I can only feel about 10 percent of my body's surface area. Since quadriplegics' natural, temperature-sensing thermostats are broken, they can no longer regulate their bodies' reaction to the ambient environment. We have found cooling less of a problem than heating. One way we solved that in our new home was with a see-through fireplace between the living room and bedroom. Now when I get cold, we can turn on the fireplace and have the additional advantage of ambience.

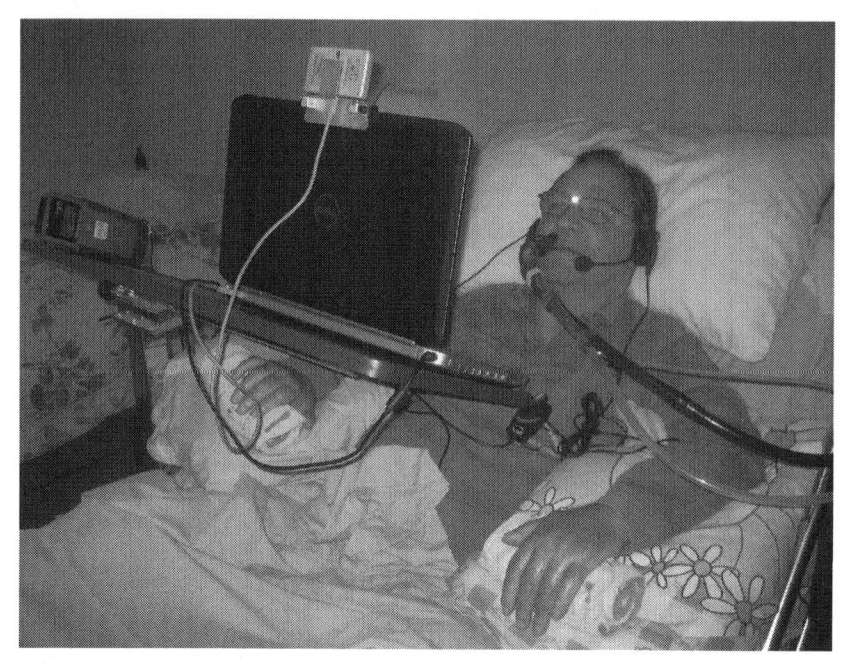

Working from bed

Roy Campanella lived a full, productive life after his injury working in the Dodger organization, but I'm sure he would have been nothing short of flabbergasted by the technology available to those in his condition only a few short years after his death.

12

THE FOUNDATION

According to the National Spinal Cord Injury Statistical Center at the University of Alabama Birmingham, only 35 percent of spinal cord injury patients are employed twenty years or more after their injury. As a result 75 percent of households with a paralyzed person report annual income of less than forty thousand dollars per year, and 65 percent of households report less than thirty thousand dollars per year, according to the United States Census. These are the individuals who cannot afford to remodel their bathrooms, purchase handicapped-accessible vans, or access many other needed items not provided by insurance. I knew what I wanted to do. I just had to figure out how to make it happen.

In late summer 2009, I received the equipment I needed to make the foundation happen. It came in the form of voice-activated computer software (Dragon Naturally Speaking Professional). What an unbelievable difference that has made in my life. With this software I can use the Internet, any Microsoft Office software, or any other software that interfaces with Dragon. This innovation allows me to pursue my passion for writing, which was something I had always wanted to do but never had the time for. About the time

I received Dragon, I also received the Sip-and-Puff assistive technology that allowed me to communicate with my voice-activated phone. Now I could call anyone I wanted without someone else having to dial and hang up. That is literally life-changing! With this equipment I began implementing my plan. I called some old, trusted industry friends to pitch the idea for a foundation. I wanted to see if they would help make it a reality by serving on the board. They wholeheartedly agreed and embraced the idea with both arms. Without their involvement nothing would have happened, and I am deeply indebted to them for their friendship, love, and support. During the fall of 2009 we filed documents with the IRS to attain 501(c) (3) status. We wanted to provide financial assistance to those with a connection to the construction trades who were living with life-altering disabilities. We wanted to provide the type of benefit we had received from the Joey Wilkins Foundation and Grapevine AMBUCS. We also wanted our website to be a one-stop resource for those seeking the kind of information we found so difficult to come by following my injury. By the end of the year, we were all ready to go, but we lacked one important ingredient—money.

In May 2010 we held our first ever foundation golf tournament fundraiser in Dallas and drew fifty-nine golfers. Following this it was seven months before we received our first application for assistance, despite our campaign for awareness. It came from an individual whose story typifies those we have come to see in every application we receive. This lady owned a plumbing contracting business with her husband and had become paralyzed in an automobile accident earlier that year. As a result they lost half their income, and bills were mounting. All their durable medical equipment and assistive technology had to be paid for out-of-pocket, and they were seeking a handicapped-accessible vehicle. Close your eyes for a minute, and put yourself in this situation. Imagine what such a gift would mean to you. We didn't have to imagine. We had been the beneficiary of such kindness through our friends and the Joey Wilkins Foundation.

Once that first assistance request came in to the foundation, it didn't take seven months for the next one. I can't help but think about one family whom the foundation helped in 2011 with a bathroom remodel. It was for a general contractor. He was about my age and had taken a fall on his bike, hitting his head on the pavement. He was able to shake it off and continue riding his bicycle, only to collapse later that day with a severe brain bleed, which left him mentally incapacitated. His accident also happened in 2008. In 2011 Baylor requested our foundation be part of a group making presentations about their services to individuals going through the same rehab I had been through. It turned out an individual in that group had ties to the construction trades and was simply looking to replace the carpet in his house with tile. A paraplegic for years, he had to roll his wheelchair over carpet, which was severely aggravating the arthritis in his shoulders. Able-bodied individuals often don't notice little things that represent big obstacles for those with disabilities. I know I didn't before, but I could relate to this individual after seeing Sue struggle to push my Hoyer lift across carpet. A Hoyer lift is an assistive device that allows a patient to be transferred between a bed and a chair. Imagine the difficulty of pushing such a device on any carpeted surface.

Our foundation is unique in that it is the only one I am aware of completely dedicated to helping those with ties to the construction trades. The power of this was never more evident than when we were contacted with a request but had very limited funds. This particular Chicago area family had gone through an indescribable sequence of tragedies and desperately needed a home and bath remodel to accommodate the needs of a woman living with the effects of a brain aneurysm. Contacts pursued by the foundation yielded a plumbing contractor who was also willing to act as the general contractor for the project. This contractor found other people to donate their labor for every aspect of the job. The foundation paid for the materials, and the entire project was completed for only a fraction of its retail cost. Just that would have been an amazing story, but there was more. A tile contractor who had donated his labor had a daughter who had suffered a brain bleed at birth and who is living with cerebral palsy and cortical blindness. It was difficult and dangerous, especially in the winter, to physically pick up her wheelchair and carry it up and down the steps to their home. Following a golf tournament fundraiser, the foundation was able to fund the installation of an outdoor elevator for him and his daughter. Our "Chicago connection" also proved helpful for one other family. The Titus representative in Chicago contacted me to see if we could help the family of a service technician who worked for a local mechanical contractor. The service technician's son had been living with cerebral palsy since birth, and his family had always lifted the child into and out of a vehicle for transportation. The son was now going into high school, and the family needed a handicapped-accessible van to transport him. New vehicles of this type run about sixty thousand dollars and are unaffordable for many. A handicapped vehicle provider stepped in to help. He found a reliable, used vehicle, while private donations were sought. That still left the family significantly short, but grants from the state of Illinois and our foundation enabled the family to procure the vehicle. In these situations vehicles represent so much more than transportation. For this young man, it meant he could go to school dances, football games, and other school events with his friends without placing an undue burden on the family. For the family it represented a huge increase in their son's independence as well as the increased safety of not having to lift him in and out of the car.

Since our inception we have received requests from individuals who found out about us through the Christopher & Dana Reeve Foundation and the Miami Project, a foundation established by Nick Buoniconti and his son. Nick was a player on the 1972 Miami Dolphins, which was the only NFL team to win the Super Bowl with a perfect seventeen and zero season. The Miami Project was founded after Nick's son was paralyzed in a college football

THE FOUNDATION

game. The two people who found us through the Miami Project both sought rehabilitative equipment. One was from California, and the other was from Chicago. Individuals also heard about us through others in the trade, from friends of the foundation, from our involvement at Comfort Tech (a major gathering of the HVAC and plumbing industry for educational seminars and product displays), through Internet surfing, and from a personal appearance at the Baylor Institute of Rehabilitation. Things were clearly evolving, and by the end of 2012, we were receiving requests faster than our ability to meet them. New strategies were needed.

At the beginning of 2013, the board held its first strategic planning meeting. Everyone felt the passion and desire to do something about the inability to meet all requests. Together we affirmed that the foundation was a journey with a purpose, but it was the impact made by the journey that counted. The golf tournament in 2013 featured 120 golfers, and we had increased corporate sponsorship. We had also been hosting a booth at Comfort Tech, which was becoming an increasingly important funding source. By the end of 2013, the foundation had assisted a total of sixteen individuals acquire truly life-changing items. More specifically, donors have made it possible for the foundation to provide six individuals with transportation solutions, seven individuals with home and bath remodels, and three individuals with assistive or adaptive technology. Among the sixteen individuals, represented trades include plumbing, HVAC, electrical, general contracting, and heavy equipment or road construction. What these grants really provide, however, is independence, which is something that can only be appreciated after it has been lost. One such recipient said it best when she wrote, "This is a wonderful foundation which provides very real and needed help."

We define our foundation not in terms of size but in terms of impact. The ultimate destination is the point where we are able to fund every properly vetted request within thirty days of approval. We realize that destination is a moving target because (A) the need is so boundless, and (B) the more impactful we are, the greater awareness will be. Therein lies the opportunity. We want to make a maximally substantial and immediate difference in the lives of as many individuals living with life-altering disabilities as we possibly can.

In the fifth year of my "internship" with a life-altering disability, I can say my life has been immensely enriched by the people I have met along the way. I have seen the silent philanthropy of people who want no public credit for their generosity. I am much more attuned to the numerous and sometimes severe medical difficulties many people live with, yet their inner spirit moves their focus upward and outward. During the course of this journey, we have discovered some amazing and talented people. I read the stories about the incredible achievements of ordinary people who do extraordinary things. This includes Brooke Ellison, the vent-dependent quadriplegic woman who graduated from Harvard, went on to get a PhD, and ran for the New York Senate. Another example is Travis Roy, rendered a quadriplegic while playing college hockey, who has raised millions of dollars for spinal cord research. When faced with major obstacles, every day is a choice. While some days are easier than others, one must reaffirm their commitment to not look back, not give up, and remain positive every single day!

To learn more about our foundation and how to become a part of it, visit us at http://www.josephgrohfoundation.org/. One hundred percent of the proceeds from this book will go to the foundation. We look forward to having you join us on our journey.

THE FOUNDATION

Foundation Board of Directors, from L to R Sue, Mike Hajaduk, Eric, David Heimer, Vicki Laplant, my sister Sue, John Laplant

About the Author

Joseph Groh was employed in the HVAC (heating, ventilation, and air-conditioning) industry for thirty-five years before being rendered a C3-C4 quadriplegic (paralyzed below the shoulders) following a 2008 bicycle accident. Over the years Joe was a sales and marketing executive with Lennox Industries, Excelsior Manufacturing, and Titus. At the time of his injury, he was vice president of sales and marketing for PCI, Inc., a manufacturer of louvers, fire/smoke/air control dampers, and acoustical and architectural products. These various industry appointments took Joe and his family from Chicago to Columbus, Ohio, Charlotte, North Carolina, and Dallas/Fort Worth, Texas.

Following his accident Joe endeavored to give back to an industry that has been so prolific in the life of his family. His grandfather, great uncle, father, uncle, aunt, cousin, sister, brother, and two sons have all made or are making their living in the construction trades industry. That led Joe to start the Joseph Groh Foundation in 2009, a 501(c) (3) organization dedicated to providing financial assistance to those with connections to the construction trades industry and who are living with life-altering disabilities. For more information visit http://www.josephgrohfoundation.org/.

Joe and his wife, Sue, live in the Dallas/Fort Worth area and have three children: Steve, Eric, and Christie.

References

"Joe Groh's life story is truly remarkable. It will amaze you, and it will inspire you. I can't imagine a person with greater proactivity than Joe! My father always taught, 'Between stimulus and response there is a space. In this space, people can choose their own response to what happens to them.' Joe's response—never look back, never give up, remain positive—is extraordinary. This book beautifully tells his story. The best part is the end of the book which shows how Joe is now not only inspiring others through his response, but how he is also now empowering others through his contributions. Talk about making a difference! Joe Groh is a force for good in this nation and in this world."

> Stephen M. R. Covey, *The New York Times* and # 1 *Wall Street Journal* bestselling author of *The Speed of Trust* and coauthor of *Smart Trust*

"some of us may have had friends that became paralyzed, but almost all of us have wondered what it would be like if it happened to us! This book describes the experience, and how ones family and faith are the basis for our world view...especially in situations of extreme stress facing an unknown future. I hope you enjoy this inspiring story of overcoming adversity ! "

> *David Weekley, Chairman of David Weekley Homes*

This is a story about a family coming together in the face of tragedy. Their story embodies a spirit emblematic of many who work in our profession. I highly recommend this inspirational book.

Scott Boxer, CEO Service Experts

From Two Wheels to Four is certainly a story of overcoming obstacles, and Joe Groh and his family will be an inspiration to many. But more so it is about the experiences, the people, and the faith that prepare one for life's inevitable changes, from the routine to the rare. Few people will find themselves paralyzed after a bicycle accident on Father's Day, as did Joe, but many will learn that regardless of their station in life, looking forward rather than backward can turn adversity into growth and advocacy for others.

Mike Murphy, Publisher, The Air Conditioning, Heating, Refrigeration NEWS

I have known Joe since my final interview at the Chicago dealer meeting shoot for the Dave Lennox spokesperson position back in 1985. I highly recommend you read this book and get to know these remarkable people. It's a story of faith, courage and perseverance that helped Joe and his family overcome a life changing event.

Bob Tibbets, Radio and TV Spokesperson At Lennox Industries

It's been my privilege to serve as the master of ceremonies at Joe's annual charity golf tournament the past couple of years, and I've found the story of Joe and his family very uplifting. It matters not what business or occupation you might be involved in, I'm confident you'll find this book informative, impactful and inspirational.

Scott Murray, Charman/CEO at Murray Media

REFERENCES

Joe Groh's story will inspire you. Instead of being self-centered in the face of incredible trials, Joe is other-centered. Instead of focusing on what he lost, he gives thanks for what he has. Instead of focusing on what he can no longer do, Joe is focused on what he can do. Instead of anger, Joe found hope. Instead of looking for help, Joe helped others and is making a tangible difference the lives of other people confronted with life altering events. He is one of the most positive people I know and through his book and uplifting message, you can get to know him as well.

Matt Michel, CEO, The Service Roundtable

Both entertaining and very compelling!! This is a book shares in a very personal manner, all you need to know about the true importance of faith, family and friends when both tackling and taming adversity!

Darion Culbertson, Mayor – Town of Fairview, Texas

Made in United States
Orlando, FL
18 August 2023